the
modern
tagine
cookbook

the
modern
tagine

cookbook

Delicious recipes for Moroccan one-pot meals

Ghillie Başan

RYLAND PETERS & SMALL
LONDON • NEW YORK

Designer Paul Stradling
Production David Hearn
Art Director Leslie Harrington
Editorial Director Julia Charles
Publisher Cindy Richards

Indexer Hilary Bird

First published in 2019 by
Ryland Peters & Small
20–21 Jockey's Fields
London WC1R 4BW
and
341 E 116th St
New York NY 10029

www.rylandpeters.com

10

Recipe collection compiled by
Julia Charles

Text copyright © Ghillie Basan 2019

The recipes in this book have been
previously published in *Flavours of
Morocco*, *Tagine*, *Tagines and Couscous*
and *Vegetarian Tagines and Couscous*.

Design and photographs copyright
© Ryland Peters & Small 2019 (see
page 144 for a full list of picture credits)

ISBN: 978-1-78879-143-4

Printed in China

A CIP record for this book is available from
the British Library.

US Library of Congress Cataloging-in-
Publication Data has been applied for.

Notes

• Both British (Metric) and American (Imperial plus US cups)
measurements are included in these recipes for your convenience;
however it is important to work with only one set of measurements
and not alternate between the two within a recipe.

• All spoon measurements are level unless otherwise specified.

• All eggs are medium (UK) or large (US), unless specified as large,
in which case US extra-large should be used. Uncooked or partially
cooked eggs should not be served to the very old, frail, young
children, pregnant women or those with compromised immune
systems.

• Ovens should be preheated to the specified temperatures. We
recommend using an oven thermometer. If using a fan-assisted
oven, adjust temperatures according to the manufacturer's
instructions.

• When a recipe calls for the grated zest of citrus fruit, buy unwaxed
fruit and wash well before using. If you can only find treated fruit,
scrub well in warm soapy water before using.

• To sterilize preserving jars, wash them in hot, soapy water and
rinse in boiling water. Place in a large saucepan and cover with
hot water. With the saucepan lid on, bring the water to a boil and
continue boiling for 15 minutes. Turn off the heat and leave the jars
in the hot water until just before they are to be filled. Invert the jars
onto a clean dish towel to dry. Sterilize the lids for 5 minutes, by
boiling or according to the manufacturer's instructions. Jars should
be filled and sealed while they are still hot.

Contents

Introduction

A tagine is an attractive and practical earthenware pot as well as the name of an aromatic casserole dish. Rooted in the traditional Berber communities of Morocco, tagine cooking lends itself well to modern eating. You can be bold and inventive and, as the ingredients cook gently in the steam that builds up inside the conical lid, ensured of succulent results. There is a little magic to a tagine, too, as you lift off the lid and release the aroma of herbs and spices, honey and fruit, and perhaps a hint of citrus, it is a feast for the senses.

Moroccan cooking is regarded as the most exquisite and refined of the Maghreb, the North African region comprising Morocco, Tunisia and Algeria. Known as 'the land where the sun sets', the Maghreb provides a stunning geographical and culinary door to the rest of Africa, as well as a lively mix of the European and Middle Eastern influences that have shaped its culinary history. A traditional Moroccan tagine can reflect the fascinating mix of cultures that have left their mark on the cuisine: the indigenous Berbers who created the tagine cooking style; the nomadic Bedouins from the desert who brought dates and grains; the Moors expelled from Spain who relied heavily on olives and olive oil and brought with them the Andalucian flavours of paprika and herbs; the Sephardic Jews with their preserving techniques employing salt; the Arabs and Ottomans who introduced the sophisticated cuisine from the Middle East; and the culinary finesse and wine-making of the French.

Traditionally a tagine would be served as a course on its own with chunks of bread to mop up the delicious buttery, syrupy and spicy sauce, but in many modern homes it is served with couscous. On festive occasions, the classic way of serving a tagine and couscous together is to pile a huge mound of the grains in the shape of a high pyramid and to hollow out the peak to form a dip into which the tagine can be spooned. Couscous is Morocco's national dish and is of fundamental value to Moroccan culture for dietary, religious and symbolic reasons. Light and easy to digest, couscous is simple to prepare and can add to your enjoyment of a modern tagine.

Harissa

This rich, fiery paste is wonderful stuff and is essential to every kitchen in the Maghreb. It is worth making a small batch of your own (a little goes a long way!) to keep handy in the refrigerator as it is a very versatile ingredient. It can be added to many tagines and couscous dishes; it can be served as a condiment to accompany just about anything; it can be stirred into sauces and marinades; and it can be transformed into a dip for warm crusty bread by combining it with oil or yogurt. Prepared by pounding spices and fresh coriander/cilantro with dried red chillies/chiles that have been soaked in water, or chillies/chiles that have been roasted in oil, harissa imparts a distinct taste to many Moroccan dishes. Jars of ready-prepared harissa are available in North African and Middle Eastern stores, as well as in some larger supermarkets and delicatessens, or you can make your own version based on this recipe. Try varying it with fennel or caraway seeds, fresh or dried mint, ground black pepper and roasted chillies/chiles instead of dried.

12 dried red chillies/chiles (Horn or New Mexico), deseeded

1 teaspoon cumin seeds

2 teaspoons coriander seeds

1 teaspoon sea salt

3–4 garlic cloves, roughly chopped

a small bunch of fresh coriander/cilantro, finely chopped

4 tablespoons olive oil

a small sterilized jar (see page 4)

MAKES 1 SMALL JAR

Put the chillies/chiles in a bowl and pour over enough warm water to cover them. Leave them to soak for 2–3 hours, then drain and squeeze out any excess water.

Using a mortar and pestle, pound the cumin and coriander seeds to a coarse paste with the salt. Add the garlic and pound until creamy, then add the chillies and pound to a thick paste. Stir in the fresh coriander/ cilantro and bind with most of the olive oil.

Transfer the paste to a small sterilized jar and pour in the remaining oil so that there is a thin layer floating on top. It will keep well in the refrigerator for up to 1 month.

Chermoula

Prepared predominantly with fresh coriander/cilantro, lemon and chillies, chermoula lends its distinct hot, citrus flavour to many marinades, grilled dishes and vegetable tagines. Unlike the deep, fiery notes of harissa, chermoula is light and lemony with a mild burst of chilli/chile and is best prepared on the day that it will be used. Variations of this basic recipe can be found alongside some of the tagine dishes in the chapters that follow.

2–3 garlic cloves, roughly chopped

1 red chilli/chile, deseeded and roughly chopped

1–2 teaspoons cumin seeds

1 teaspoon sea salt

a big bunch of fresh coriander/cilantro leaves, finely chopped

a pinch of saffron threads, soaked in a little water

freshly squeezed juice of 1 lemon

3–4 tablespoons olive oil

MAKES A BOWL

Using a mortar and pestle, pound the garlic with the chilli/chile, cumin seeds and salt to a coarse paste. Add the chopped coriander/cilantro and pound again to as smooth a paste as you can get. Stir in the saffron, along with its soaking water, and the lemon juice and olive oil.

Ras el hanout

This traditional spice mix is so wonderfully pungent and eloquent, it could be described as poetry in a powder. Full of character, reflecting centuries of trade, war, diverse cultures and the geographical spread of Morocco's culinary history, this synthesis of spices is fiery, aromatic and warming all at the same time. Packed with strong Indian aromas of cardamom, cloves, ginger, peppercorns and mace; cinnamon from Sri Lanka; cloves from Zanzibar; local African roots and plants, such as guinea pepper from the Ivory Coast; orris root from the Atlas Mountains; and the delicate, perfumed notes of rose buds, belladonna berries, fennel flowers and lavender from Morocco and Europe, ras el hanout is as unique as the hand that makes it, as every spice merchant has his own recipe. Translated from Arabic as 'head of the shop' it is a delightfully complex medley of 30–40 different spices. Beyond the souks of Morocco, it is difficult to make an authentic ras el hanout, but you can create your own version by loosely following the recipe below, or you can order the aromatic ras el hanout produced by Seasoned Pioneers at www.seasonedpioneers.co.uk.

Using a mortar and pestle, or an electric blender, grind together all the spices to form a coarse powder.

Stir in the dried lavender and rose petals and tip the mix into an airtight container.

You can store the spice mix for about 6 months if you keep it in a cool cupboard well away from direct sunlight.

1 teaspoon black peppercorns

1 teaspoon cloves

1 teaspoon aniseed seeds

1 teaspoon nigella seeds

1 teaspoon allspice berries

1 teaspoon cardamom seeds

2 teaspoons ground ginger

2 teaspoons ground turmeric

2 teaspoons coriander seeds

2 pieces of mace

2 pieces of cinnamon bark

2 teaspoons dried mint

1 dried red chilli/chile

1 teaspoon dried lavender

6 dried rose buds, broken up

MAKES 4–5 TABLESPOONS

Smen

An acquired taste, smen is an aged butter with a rancid flavour. Often flavoured with herbs and spices and set in earthenware pots, smen can be stored in a cool, dry place for months, sometimes years. It is the primary cooking fat for many Berber communities, who also enjoy this pungent butter smeared on bread. An essential component of many traditional tagines, particularly ones with a high spice content, smen can be substituted with ghee (clarified butter), which isn't as pungent as smen but it does emit a warm, nutty aroma to the dish. Ghee (usually an Indian brand) is sold in Middle Eastern and Asian stores, as well as in some larger supermarkets, or you can try making your own version of smen.

500 g/4 sticks unsalted butter, at room temperature

1 tablespoon sea salt

1 tablespoon dried oregano

a sterilized jar (see page 4)

MAKES ABOUT 500 G/1 LB.

Soften the butter in a bowl. Put the salt and dried oregano in a saucepan with 150 ml/⅔ cup water and boil to reduce it a little. Strain the water directly onto the butter and stir with a wooden spoon to make sure it is well blended, then leave to cool.

Knead the butter with your hands to bind it, squeezing out any excess water. Drain well and spoon the butter into the prepared jar. Seal the jar and store it in a cool, dry place for at least 6 weeks before using in a recipe.

Preserved lemons

Small, thin-skinned lemons native to the Maghreb are traditionally preserved in salt and lemon juice to impart a distinctive, citrus flavour to many tagines, grilled dishes and salads. Generally, it is only the rind, finely chopped or sliced, that is employed in the dishes as the flesh is too salty. The refreshing, tangy taste of these preserved lemons is unique and is essential to the cooking of many traditional tagines, particularly vegetable ones. You can buy jars of ready-preserved lemons in Middle Eastern and North African stores, as well as some supermarkets and delicatessens, but they are easy to make at home.

10 organic, unwaxed lemons, plus the juice of 3–4 lemons

about 10 tablespoons sea salt

a large sterilized jar (see page 4)

MAKES A LARGE JAR

Wash and dry the lemons and slice one of the ends off each lemon. Stand each lemon on the flattened end and make two vertical cuts three-quarters of the way through them, as if cutting them into quarters but keeping the base intact. Stuff a tablespoon of salt into each lemon and pack them into the prepared jar. Store the jar of lemons in a cool place for 3–4 days to soften the skins.

After this time, press the lemons down into the jar, so they are even more tightly packed. Pour the lemon juice over the salted lemons, until they are completely covered. Seal the jar and store it in a cool place for at least a month.

To use, rinse the salt off the preserved lemons and pat them dry. Using a small sharp knife, cut the lemons into quarters lengthways and remove all the flesh and pith so that you are just left with the rind. Finely slice or chop the rind according to the recipe.

meat & poultry

Classic lamb tagine with almonds, prunes and apricots

This is perhaps the best known of all Moroccan tagines. Aromatic, sweet, succulent and juicy with the addition of the fruit, this is a perfect introduction to the tastes of Morocco. Traditionally this dish would be served with bread to mop up the syrupy sauce, or you can serve it with couscous.

1–2 tablespoons olive oil

2 tablespoons blanched almonds

2 red onions, finely chopped

2–3 garlic cloves, finely chopped

a thumb-sized piece of fresh ginger, peeled and chopped

a pinch of saffron threads

2 cinnamon sticks

1–2 teaspoons coriander seeds, crushed

500 g/1 lb. 2 oz. boned lamb, from the shoulder, leg or shanks, trimmed and cubed

about 12 stoned prunes and 6 dried apricots, soaked in cold water for 1 hour and drained

3–4 strips orange rind

1–2 tablespoons dark honey

a handful of fresh coriander/cilantro leaves, chopped

sea salt and freshly ground black pepper

bread or Plain Buttery Couscous (see page 120), to serve

SERVES 4–6

Heat the oil in the base of a tagine or a heavy-based casserole. Add the almonds and cook, stirring, until they turn golden. Add the onions and garlic and sauté until they begin to colour. Stir in the ginger, saffron, cinnamon sticks and coriander seeds. Toss the lamb into the tagine and sauté for 1–2 minutes, stirring to make sure it is coated in the onion and spices.

Pour in enough water to just cover the meat, then bring it to the boil. Reduce the heat, put the lid on the tagine and simmer for 1 hour, until the meat is tender. Add the prunes, apricots and orange rind, put the lid on the tagine again, and simmer for a further 15–20 minutes.

Stir in the honey, season with salt and pepper, cover, and simmer for a further 10 minutes. Make sure there is enough liquid in the pot as you want the sauce to be syrupy and slightly caramelized, but not dry. Stir in half of the fresh coriander/cilantro, then serve immediately, sprinkled with the remaining coriander/cilantro and accompanied by chunks of crusty bread or a mound of Plain, Buttery Couscous.

Lamb tagine with chestnuts, saffron and pomegranate seeds

This is a lovely winter dish, decorated with ruby-red pomegranate seeds. Whole, meaty chestnuts are often used in Arab-influenced culinary cultures as a substitute for potatoes. You can use freshly roasted nuts or ready-peeled, vacuum-packed or frozen chestnuts.

2 tablespoons ghee

2 onions, finely chopped

4 garlic cloves, finely chopped

a thumb-sized piece of fresh ginger, peeled and finely chopped or shredded

a pinch of saffron threads

1–2 cinnamon sticks

1 kg/2 lb. 4 oz. lean lamb, from the shoulder or leg, trimmed and cut into bite-sized pieces

250 g/1 cup peeled chestnuts

1–2 tablespoons dark, runny honey

sea salt and freshly ground black pepper

seeds of 1 pomegranate, pith removed

a small bunch of fresh mint leaves, chopped

a small bunch of fresh coriander/cilantro leaves, chopped

bread or Plain Buttery Couscous (see page 120), to serve

SERVES 4

Heat the ghee in a tagine or a heavy-based casserole. Stir in the onions, garlic and ginger and sauté until they begin to colour. Add the saffron and cinnamon sticks, and toss in the lamb. Pour in enough water to almost cover the meat and bring it to the boil. Reduce the heat, cover with a lid and simmer gently for about 1 hour.

Add the chestnuts and stir in the honey. Cover with the lid again and cook gently for a further 30 minutes, until the meat is very tender. Season to taste with salt and plenty of black pepper and then toss in some of the pomegranate seeds, mint and coriander/cilantro. Sprinkle the remaining pomegranate seeds and herbs over the lamb, and serve with bread or Plain Buttery Couscous (see page 120).

Summer tagine of lamb, courgettes, peppers and mint

Summer tagines using seasonal vegetables are often quite light and colourful. Other vegetables that might be added to this tagine include tomatoes, aubergines/eggplants and peas. This dish is particularly good served with wedges of lemon to squeeze over it, or with finely shredded preserved lemon (see page 13) sprinkled over the top.

3–4 tablespoons olive oil

1 onion, roughly chopped

4 garlic cloves, roughly chopped

1 teaspoon cumin seeds

1 teaspoon coriander seeds

1 teaspoon dried mint

a thumb-sized piece of fresh ginger, peeled and finely chopped or grated

750 g/1 lb. 10 oz. lean lamb, cut into bite-sized pieces

sea salt and freshly ground black pepper

2 small courgettes/zucchini, sliced thickly on the diagonal

1 red or green (bell) pepper, deseeded and cut into thick strips

4 tomatoes, skinned, deseeded and cut into chunks

a small bunch of fresh flat-leaf parsley, roughly chopped

a small bunch of fresh mint leaves, roughly chopped

1 lemon, cut into quarters, to serve

SERVES 4–6

Heat the olive oil in a tagine or a heavy-based casserole. Stir in the onion, garlic, cumin and coriander seeds, dried mint and ginger. Once the onions begin to soften, toss in the meat and pour in enough water to just cover it. Bring the water to the boil, reduce the heat, cover with a lid and cook gently for about 1½ hours.

Season the cooking juices with salt and pepper. Add the courgettes/zucchini, (bell) pepper and tomatoes, tucking them around the meat (add a little more water if necessary). Cover with a lid again and cook for about 15 minutes, until the courgettes/zucchini and pepper are cooked but retain a bite.

Toss in some of the chopped parsley and fresh mint, sprinkle the rest over the top and serve immediately with lemon wedges to squeeze over the dish.

This summery tagine is best accompanied by a fresh green salad of young beetroot/beets, spinach and lettuce leaves.

Lamb tagine with shallots and dates

Commonly known as the 'bread of the desert', dates are treated as a sacred food source by the Arabs and the Berbers as they and their ancestors have survived off them for generations, even when there has been little else to eat. They also symbolize hospitality and prosperity, so they are offered to guests and they are popped into numerous tagines and couscous dishes.

3 tablespoons olive oil with a knob of butter, or ghee

700 g/1 lb. 9 oz. lean boned lamb, from the shoulder or neck, trimmed and cubed

12 shallots, peeled and left whole

4–6 garlic cloves, peeled and left whole

2 teaspoons ground turmeric

2 cinnamon sticks

1–2 tablespoons runny honey

225 g/1¾ cups pitted moist dates

1–2 tablespoons sesame seeds, toasted

sea salt and freshly ground black pepper

bread or Plain Buttery Couscous (see page 120), to serve

SERVES 4–6

Heat the oil and the butter in the base of a tagine or a heavy-based casserole. Toss the lamb in and brown it all over. Using a slotted spoon, remove the meat from the tagine and set aside. Add the shallots and garlic and sauté, stirring occasionally, until they begin to colour. Add the turmeric and cinnamon sticks and return the meat to the tagine. Pour in just enough water to cover the meat, then bring it to the boil. Reduce the heat, cover with the lid and simmer for about 1 hour, giving it a stir from time to time.

Stir in the honey and season with salt and lots of black pepper. Add the dates, replace the lid, and cook for a further 25–30 minutes. Sprinkle with the toasted sesame seeds and serve with chunks of crusty bread or a large mound of Plain Buttery Couscous.

Baked lamb tagine with quinces, figs and honey

1.5 kg/3¼ lb. shoulder of lamb on the bone

2 tablespoons ghee

2 red onions, cut into wedges

225 g/1¾ cups ready-to-eat prunes, pitted

225 g/1¾ cups ready-to-eat dried figs, or fresh figs, halved

40 g/3 tablespoons butter

2 fresh quinces, quartered and cored (soak in water with a squeeze of lemon juice until ready to use)

2 tablespoons orange blossom water

2 tablespoons dark, runny honey

a bunch of fresh flat-leaf parsley, chopped

a bunch of fresh coriander/cilantro, chopped

For the chermoula

4 garlic cloves, chopped

a large thumb-sized piece of fresh ginger, peeled and chopped

1 red chilli/chile, deseeded and chopped

1 teaspoon sea salt

a small bunch of fresh coriander/cilantro, chopped

a small bunch of fresh flat-leaf parsley, chopped

2–3 teaspoons ground coriander

2–3 teaspoons ground cumin

3 tablespoons olive oil

2 tablespoons dark, runny honey

freshly squeezed juice of 1 lemon

SERVES 4–6

In this festive dish, a shoulder of lamb is marinated in chermoula – a Moroccan herb and spice mix – and baked slowly. You can use apples or pears instead of quinces. Buttery couscous (see page 120) or roasted potatoes and a leafy salad are good accompaniments.

First, make the chermoula. Using a mortar and pestle, pound the garlic, ginger, chilli/chile and salt to form a coarse paste. Add the fresh coriander/cilantro and parsley and pound into the paste. Beat in the ground coriander and cumin, and bind with the olive oil, honey and lemon juice (alternatively, you can whizz all the ingredients in an electric blender). Cut small incisions in the shoulder of lamb with a sharp knife and rub the chermoula well into the meat. Cover and leave in the refrigerator for at least 6 hours, or overnight.

Preheat the oven to 180°C (350°F) Gas 4.

Heat the ghee in a tagine or a heavy-based casserole, add the lamb and brown it all over. Transfer the meat to a plate. Stir the onions and any leftover chermoula into the ghee. Add the prunes and if using dried figs, add them at this stage. Pour in 300 ml/1¼ cups water and put the lamb back into the tagine. Cover with the lid and put the tagine in the oven for about 2 hours.

Towards the end of the cooking time, melt the butter in a heavy-based pan, toss in the quinces and sauté until golden brown. Remove the tagine from the oven and place the quince around the meat (if using fresh figs, add them at this stage). Splash the orange blossom water over the lamb and drizzle the honey over the meat and the fruit. Return the tagine to the oven for a further 25–30 minutes, until the meat and fruit are nicely browned and the lamb is so tender it almost falls off the bone. Sprinkle the chopped parsley and coriander/cilantro over the top and serve immediately.

Chicken tagine with preserved lemons, green olives and thyme

This is another Moroccan classic employing two of the most traditional ingredients: cracked green olives and preserved lemon. Refreshing and tasty, this dish can be made with chicken joints or a whole chicken. Served with a lemon couscous and a side salad or vegetable dish, such as steamed carrots tossed with spices and mint, this is a delicious dish for lunch or supper.

1 organic chicken, about 1.5 kg/ 3¼ lb.

1 tablespoon olive oil with a knob of butter

2 preserved lemons (see page 13), cut into strips

175 g/1¾ cups cracked green olives

1–2 teaspoons dried thyme or oregano

a small bunch of fresh flat-leaf parsley, finely chopped

bread or Lemon Couscous (see page 128), to serve

For the marinade

1 onion, grated

3 garlic cloves, crushed

a thumb-sized piece of fresh ginger, peeled and grated

a small bunch of fresh coriander/ cilantro, finely chopped

a pinch of saffron threads

freshly squeezed juice of 1 lemon

3–4 tablespoons olive oil

sea salt and freshly ground black pepper

SERVES 4–6

In a bowl mix together all the ingredients for the marinade and rub it all over the inside and outside of the chicken. Cover and chill in the refrigerator for 1–2 hours.

Heat the olive oil and butter in the base of a tagine or a heavy-based casserole. Add the chicken and brown it on all sides. Tip in any leftover marinade and add enough water to come halfway up the sides of the chicken. Bring the water to the boil, reduce the heat and cover with a lid. Simmer for about 50 minutes, turning the chicken from time to time.

Add the preserved lemons, olives and half of the thyme. Cover with the lid again and simmer for a further 20 minutes. Check the seasoning and add some salt and pepper if necessary. Sprinkle the rest of the thyme and the parsley over the top. Serve from the tagine with fresh, crusty bread or Lemon Couscous and a salad or vegetable dish.

Spicy chicken tagine with apricots, rosemary and ginger

This tagine is both fruity and spicy, and the rosemary and ginger give it a delightful aroma. It can be made with chicken joints or pigeon breasts, pheasant or duck, and needs only a buttery couscous (see page 120) and a leafy salad to accompany it.

2 tablespoons olive oil with a knob of butter

1 onion, finely chopped

3 sprigs of rosemary, 1 finely chopped, the other 2 cut in half

a large thumb-sized piece of fresh ginger, peeled and finely chopped

2 red chillies/chiles, deseeded and finely chopped

1–2 cinnamon sticks

8 chicken thighs

175 g/generous 1 cup ready-to-eat dried apricots

2 tablespoons clear honey

1 x 400-g/14-oz. can of plum tomatoes with their juice

sea salt and freshly ground black pepper

a small bunch of fresh green or purple basil leaves

SERVES 4

Heat the oil and butter in a tagine or a heavy-based casserole. Stir in the onion, chopped rosemary, ginger and chillies/chiles and sauté until the onion begins to soften. Stir in the halved rosemary sprigs and the cinnamon sticks. Add the chicken thighs and brown them on both sides. Toss in the apricots with the honey, then stir in the plum tomatoes with their juice. (Add a little water if necessary, to ensure there is enough liquid to cover the base of the tagine and submerge the apricots.) Bring the liquid to the boil, then reduce the heat. Cover with a lid and cook gently for 35–40 minutes.

Season to taste with salt and pepper. Shred the larger basil leaves and leave the small ones intact. Sprinkle them over the chicken and serve the dish immediately.

Chicken tagine with harissa, artichokes and green grapes

With the tangy notes of preserved lemon (see page 13) combined with the sweet grapes, this tagine is deliciously refreshing. It is best accompanied by buttery couscous (see page 120) or flatbread and a leafy salad. You can use ready-prepared artichoke hearts or bottoms, which are available frozen or canned.

4 chicken breasts, cut into thick strips or chunks

2 tablespoons olive oil

2 onions, halved lengthways and sliced with the grain

½ preserved lemon (see page 13), thinly sliced

1–2 teaspoons sugar

1–2 teaspoons harissa (see page 8)

2 teaspoons tomato paste

300 ml/1¼ cups chicken stock or water

1 x 400-g/14-oz. can of artichoke hearts, drained, rinsed and halved

about 16 fresh green grapes, halved lengthways

a bunch of fresh coriander/cilantro leaves, coarsely chopped

sea salt and freshly ground black pepper

For the marinade

2 garlic cloves, crushed

1 teaspoon ground turmeric

freshly squeezed juice of 1 lemon

1 tablespoon olive oil

SERVES 4–6

First, make the marinade. In a bowl, mix together the garlic, turmeric, lemon juice and olive oil. Toss the chicken in the mixture, then cover and leave in the refrigerator to marinate for 1–2 hours.

Heat the oil in a tagine or a heavy-based casserole. Stir in the onions, preserved lemon and the sugar and sauté for 2–3 minutes, until slightly caramelized. Toss in the marinated chicken, then add the harissa and tomato paste. Pour in the stock and bring it to the boil. Reduce the heat, cover with a lid and cook gently for 15 minutes.

Toss in the artichoke hearts, cover with the lid again and cook for a further 5 minutes. Add the grapes with some of the coriander/cilantro and season to taste with salt and pepper. Sprinkle with the remaining coriander/cilantro to serve.

Duck tagine with pears and cinnamon

This traditional tagine can be prepared with duck, chicken, poussin or quails. Variations of the recipe can include quince, plums, apples, cherries and apricots. Serve the tagine with bread to mop up the syrupy juices or with Plain Buttery Couscous.

2 tablespoons olive oil, plus a knob of butter

2 onions, finely chopped

a thumb-sized piece of fresh ginger, peeled and finely chopped

2 cinnamon sticks

a pinch of saffron threads

1 kg/2 lb. 4 oz. duck meat, from the thigh, breast or leg, off the bone and cut into bite-sized pieces

2 tablespoons butter

3–4 tablespoons clear, runny honey

3 pears, peeled, quartered and cored

2–3 tablespoons orange blossom water

sea salt and freshly ground black pepper

1–2 tablespoons toasted sesame seeds

a few lemon balm leaves, to garnish (optional)

crusty bread or Plain Buttery Couscous (see page 120), to serve

SERVES 4–6

Heat the oil and butter in a tagine or a heavy-based saucepan. Add the onions and ginger and sauté until they begin to colour, then add the cinnamon sticks and saffron. Toss in the duck meat, making sure it is well coated in the ginger and onions. Pour in roughly 600 ml/2½ cups water and bring it to the boil. Reduce the heat, cover and simmer gently for about 40 minutes, until the duck is tender.

Meanwhile, melt the butter in a heavy-based saucepan and stir in the honey. Toss in the pears and cook gently until they begin to caramelize. Add the pears to the duck with the orange blossom water and cook the tagine for a further 10 minutes.

Season to taste with salt and pepper and scatter the toasted sesame seeds over the top. Garnish with lemon balm leaves, if using, and serve with crusty bread or Plain Buttery Couscous.

Chorizo tagine with lentils and fenugreek

This is very simple yet delicious peasant food. Prepared with locally-cured, spicy Moroccan merguez sausages or chorizo and lentils or beans, it is a satisfying dish, best served with flatbreads and a generous dollop of creamy yogurt.

2 tablespoons olive oil

2 onions, chopped

2 garlic cloves, chopped

450 g/1 lb. chorizo or merguez sausage, thickly sliced

2 teaspoons ground turmeric

2 teaspoons ground fenugreek

225 g/1¼ cups brown lentils

a 400-g/14-oz. can of chopped tomatoes

2 teaspoons sugar

leaves from a bunch of fresh coriander/cilantro, roughly chopped (reserve some to garnish)

sea salt and freshly ground black pepper

warmed flatbreads and natural yogurt, to serve

SERVES 4–6

Heat the oil in a tagine or a heavy-based casserole.

Add the onions and garlic and sauté until they begin to colour. Toss in the chorizo slices and sauté for 1–2 minutes just to flavour the oil. Stir in the turmeric and fenugreek and add the lentils, making sure they are well coated with the spices.

Add the tomatoes with the sugar and pour in enough water to cover the lentils by 2.5 cm/1 inch. Bring the liquid to the boil, reduce the heat, put on the lid and cook gently for about 25 minutes, adding more water if necessary, until the lentils are tender but not mushy.

Toss in the coriander/cilantro and season to taste with salt and pepper. Scatter the rest of the coriander/cilantro over the top and serve with warmed flatbreads and natural yogurt.

Beef tagine with beetroot and oranges

Earthy and fruity, with a hint of ginger, this tagine is a good winter warmer. It can be made with either fresh or pre-cooked beetroot/beets. You could also serve roasted pumpkin or butternut squash and Plain Buttery Couscous (see page 120) tossed with pistachios or pine nuts.

1–2 tablespoons ghee

3–4 garlic cloves, crushed

1 red onion, halved lengthways and sliced with the grain

a large thumb-sized piece of fresh ginger, peeled and finely chopped or grated

1 red chilli/chile, deseeded and sliced

2 teaspoons coriander seeds, crushed

2 cinnamon sticks

3–4 beetroots/beets, peeled and quartered

500 g/1 lb. 2 oz. lean beef, cut into bite-sized cubes or strips

2 thin-skinned oranges, cut into segments

1 tablespoon dark, runny honey

1–2 tablespoons orange blossom water

sea salt and freshly ground black pepper

a knob of butter

2–3 tablespoons shelled pistachio nuts

a small bunch of fresh flat-leaf parsley, roughly chopped

SERVES 4–6

Melt the ghee in a tagine or a heavy-based casserole, and stir in the garlic, onion and ginger until they begin to colour. Add the chilli/chile, coriander seeds and cinnamon sticks. Add the beetroot/beets and sauté for 2–3 minutes. Toss in the beef and sauté for 1 minute. Pour in enough water to almost cover the beef and beetroot/beets and bring it to the boil. Reduce the heat, cover with a lid and simmer for 1 hour, until the meat is very tender.

Add the orange segments, honey and orange blossom water to the tagine and season the dish with salt and pepper to taste. Cover with the lid and cook for a further 10–15 minutes.

Melt the butter in a small saucepan and toss in the pistachio nuts, stirring them over medium heat until they turn golden brown. Sprinkle them over the tagine along with the flat-leaf parsley and serve.

Beef tagine with sweet potatoes, peas, ginger and ras el hanout

This fairly fiery dish is laced with the powerful flavours and aromas of ras el hanout (see page 11), a traditional spice mix. Regional variations use turnip, yam, pumpkin or butternut squash instead of sweet potatoes. The tagine is best served with Plain Buttery Couscous (see page 120) or chunks of bread and cooling yogurt or a glass of mint tea.

2 tablespoons ghee or olive oil

a large thumb-sized piece of fresh ginger, peeled and finely shredded

1 onion, finely chopped

1 kg/2 lb. 4 oz. lean beef, cubed

1–2 teaspoons ras el hanout (see page 11)

2 medium sweet potatoes, peeled and cubed

sea salt and freshly ground black pepper

500 g/1 lb. 2 oz. shelled fresh peas or frozen peas

2–3 tomatoes, skinned, deseeded and chopped

1 preserved lemon (see page 13), finely shredded or chopped

a small bunch of fresh coriander/cilantro leaves, finely chopped

SERVES 4

Heat the ghee in a tagine or a heavy-based casserole. Stir in the ginger and onion and sauté until soft. Toss in the beef and sear it on all sides, then stir in the ras el hanout. Pour in enough water to just cover the meat mixture and bring it to the boil. Reduce the heat, cover with the lid and cook gently for about 40 minutes.

Add the sweet potato to the tagine, season with salt and pepper to taste, cover with the lid and cook gently for a further 20 minutes, until the meat is tender. Toss in the peas and tomatoes, cover with the lid and cook for 5–10 minutes.

Sprinkle the preserved lemon and the coriander/cilantro over the top and serve.

fish & shellfish

Monkfish tagine with preserved lemon and mint

2–3 tablespoons olive oil

1 red onion, finely chopped

2 carrots, finely chopped

2 celery stalks, finely chopped

1 preserved lemon (see page 13), finely chopped

1 x 400-g/14-oz can of plum tomatoes with their juice

300 ml/1¼ cups fish stock or water

1 kg/2 lb. 4 oz. fresh monkfish tail, cut into large chunks

a bunch of fresh mint leaves, finely shredded

sea salt and freshly ground black pepper

bread or sautéed potatoes, to serve

For the chermoula

2–3 garlic cloves, chopped

1 red chilli/chile, deseeded and chopped

1 teaspoon sea salt

a small bunch of fresh coriander/cilantro

a pinch of saffron threads

1–2 teaspoons ground cumin

3–4 tablespoons olive oil

freshly squeezed juice of 1 lemon

SERVES 4–6

Fresh fish tagines of the coastal areas are simply wonderful, redolent with spices and buttery sauces, often piquant with lemon and chillies/chiles and tempered with fresh herbs. Inland, fish tagines are made with freshwater fish, such as the local shad, and flavoured with the herbs of the region. The distinct Moroccan marinade, chermoula, is often employed in fish dishes as the flavours of chilli/chile, cumin and coriander/cilantro marry so well and complement the fish perfectly. Serve this tagine with chunks of fresh bread, or sautéed potatoes and a leafy salad.

First make the chermoula. Using a mortar and pestle pound the garlic and chilli/chile with the salt to form a paste. Add the coriander/cilantro leaves and pound to a coarse paste. Beat in the saffron threads and cumin and bind well with the olive oil and lemon juice (you can whizz all the ingredients together in an electric blender, if you prefer). Reserve 2 teaspoons of the chermoula for cooking. Toss the monkfish in the remaining chermoula, cover and leave to marinate in the refrigerator for 1–2 hours.

Heat the oil in the base of a tagine or a heavy-based casserole. Stir in the onion, carrots and celery and sauté for 2–3 minutes, until softened. Stir in half the preserved lemon, the reserved 2 teaspoons of chermoula and the tomatoes. Cook gently for about 10 minutes to reduce the liquid, then add the stock. Bring the liquid to the boil, cover the tagine, reduce the heat and simmer for 10–15 minutes.

Add the monkfish to the tagine, cover with the lid and cook gently for 6–8 minutes, until the fish is cooked through. Season with salt and pepper, sprinkle with the remaining preserved lemon and the shredded mint and serve with chunks of fresh bread or sautéed potatoes and a leafy salad.

Oven-baked tagine of red mullet, tomatoes and lime

Baking whole fish in a tagine keeps the flesh deliciously moist. Obviously, you need to select fish that fits snugly into your tagine. The most popular fish for oven-baking in North Africa include red mullet, sardines, red snapper, grouper and sea bass. You could serve this dish with Plain Buttery Couscous (see page 120) or a tangy salad.

2 tablespoons olive oil

25 g/2 scant tablespoons butter

2–3 garlic cloves, thinly sliced

3–4 good-sized red mullet, gutted and cleaned

sea salt

2–3 large tomatoes, thinly sliced

1 lime, thinly sliced, plus 1 lime, cut into wedges, to serve

a small bunch of fresh flat-leaf parsley, coarsely chopped

SERVES 3–4

Preheat the oven to 180°C (350°F) Gas 4.

Heat the olive oil and butter in a tagine or an ovenproof dish. Stir in the garlic and sauté until it begins to brown. Put the fish in the tagine and cook it until the skin has browned and lightly buckled. (If you are using an ovenproof dish, you can brown the garlic and fish in a frying pan/skillet first.) Turn off the heat, sprinkle a little salt over the fish and tuck the slices of tomato and lime over and around them. Cover with the lid and bake in the oven for about 15 minutes.

Remove the lid and bake for a further 5–10 minutes, until the fish is cooked and nicely browned on top (you could do this under the grill/broiler, if you prefer).

Sprinkle the parsley over the top and serve with wedges of lime to squeeze over the fish.

Prawn tagine with saffron, ginger and fennel

Many shellfish tagines are not so much traditional as they are inspired by cultural influences, such as the prawn/shrimp and mussel tagines of Tangier that resemble the cooking of Andalusia across the Mediterranean Sea. Serve this tagine as a first or second course with chunks of crusty bread.

4–5 tablespoons olive oil

20 raw king prawns/jumbo shrimp, with heads removed

2 onions, finely chopped

2 garlic cloves, finely chopped

a thumb-sized piece of fresh ginger, peeled and finely chopped

a pinch of saffron threads

1–2 teaspoons smoked paprika

1 x 400-g/14-oz can of tomatoes, drained of juice

a small bunch of fresh coriander/ cilantro, finely chopped

a small bunch of fresh flat-leaf parsley, finely chopped

1 teaspoon sugar

4 fennel bulbs, trimmed and sliced thickly lengthways

sea salt and freshly ground black pepper

bread, to serve

SERVES 4

Heat 2–3 tablespoons of the olive oil in the base of a tagine or a heavy-based casserole. Add the prawns/shrimp and cook for 2–3 minutes, until they turn opaque. Using a slotted spoon, remove the prawns/shrimp from the tagine and set aside. Keep the oil in the pan.

Stir the onion, garlic, ginger and saffron into the oil and sauté for 3–4 minutes, until they begin to colour. Add the paprika, tomatoes and half the herbs. Stir in the sugar and season with salt and pepper. Cook gently, partially covered, for about 10 minutes until the mixture thickens to form a sauce.

Meanwhile, steam the fennel for about 5 minutes, until it softens. Heat the remaining olive oil in a frying pan/skillet and add the steamed fennel. Cook gently on both sides for 4–5 minutes, until it turns golden. Sprinkle with salt and pepper.

Toss the cooked prawns/shrimp in the tomato sauce, place the fennel on top, cover with the lid, and cook gently for 5 minutes. Sprinkle with the remaining coriander/cilantro and parsley immediately before serving.

Fish and shellfish k'dra with couscous

2 tablespoons olive oil

2 teaspoons cumin seeds

2 teaspoons coriander seeds

2 teaspoons ground turmeric

1 tablespoon harissa (see page 8)

leaves from a small bunch of flat-leaf parsley, finely chopped

2 litres/quarts fish stock or water

4–6 garlic cloves, finely sliced

2 x 400-g/14-oz cans of whole plum tomatoes, drained of juice

2–3 carrots, cut into matchsticks

2–3 courgettes/zucchini, cut into matchsticks

1 kg/2 lb. 4 oz. firm-fleshed fish fillets

450 g/1 lb. uncooked prawns/shrimp, shelled and deveined

450 g/1 lb. fresh mussels, cleaned

450 g/1 lb. scallops, shelled and cleaned

sea salt and freshly ground black pepper

leaves from a small bunch of fresh coriander, finely chopped

For the couscous

350 g/2 cups couscous, rinsed and drained

400 ml/1⅝ cups warm water

2 tablespoons olive or sunflower oil

25 g/2 scant tablespoons butter, broken into little pieces

SERVES 4–6

In the coastal regions, this is the king of fish dishes. Prepared in vast quantities for a family celebration, it combines the riches of the sea and the land in one big copper pot. Any firm-fleshed fish such as haddock, trout or sea bass will work here.

Preheat the oven to 180°C (350°F) Gas 4.

Tip the couscous grains into an ovenproof dish. Stir ½ teaspoon salt into the water and pour it over the couscous. Set aside for about 20 minutes.

Meanwhile, heat the oil in a large copper pot, or very large heavy-based saucepan. Stir in the cumin and coriander seeds, turmeric and harissa. Add the parsley and pour in the fish stock. Bring the liquid to the boil, reduce the heat and simmer for 5 minutes. Add the garlic, tomatoes, carrots and courgettes/zucchini and simmer for a further 10 minutes.

Using your fingers, rub the oil into the couscous grains to break up the lumps and aerate them. Scatter the pieces of butter over the top and cover with a piece of foil or wet greaseproof paper. Place in the oven for about 15 minutes to heat through.

Add the fish and shellfish to the simmering broth and cook for 5–10 minutes, until the fish is flaky, the prawns/shrimp are opaque, and the shells of the mussels have opened (discard any that remain closed). Season to taste with salt and pepper and stir in a little coriander/cilantro.

Fluff up the couscous with a fork and pile it onto a large serving plate in a domed mound. Spoon the fish and shellfish around the couscous and drizzle with a little of the broth. Ladle the rest of the broth into individual bowls and serve immediately.

Monkfish tagine with potatoes, cherry tomatoes and black olives

Flavoured with garlic, chilli/chile, cumin and coriander/cilantro (a popular version of Morocco's favourite chermoula spice mix), this tagine can be made with any meaty white fish. Serve it as a meal in itself with fresh crusty bread to mop up the delicious juices, or with Plain Buttery Couscous (see page 120).

about 900 g/2 lb monkfish tail, cut into chunks

about 12 small new potatoes

3 tablespoons olive oil with a knob of butter

3–4 garlic cloves, thinly sliced

12–16 cherry tomatoes

2 green (bell) peppers, grilled until black, skinned and cut into strips

sea salt and freshly ground black pepper

about 12 fleshy black olives

1 lemon, cut into wedges, to serve

For the chermoula

2 garlic cloves

1 teaspoon coarse salt

1–2 teaspoons cumin seeds, crushed or ground

1 red chilli/chile, deseeded and chopped

freshly squeezed juice of 1 lemon

2 tablespoons olive oil

a small bunch of fresh coriander/cilantro, roughly chopped

SERVES 4–6

First, make the chermoula. Using a mortar and pestle, pound the garlic with the salt to a smooth paste. Add the cumin, chilli/chile, lemon juice and olive oil and stir in the coriander/cilantro. Put the fish in a shallow dish and rub it with most of the chermoula (reserve a little for cooking). Cover and leave to marinate in the refrigerator for 1–2 hours.

Meanwhile, bring a saucepan of water to the boil and drop in the potatoes. Boil vigorously for about 8 minutes to soften them a little, then drain and refresh under cold running water. Peel and cut them in half lengthways.

Heat 2 tablespoons olive oil with the butter in a tagine or a heavy-based saucepan. Stir in the garlic and, when it begins to brown, add the tomatoes to soften them. Add the skinned (bell) peppers and the reserved chermoula, and season to taste with salt and pepper. Tip the mixture onto a plate.

Arrange the potatoes over the base of the tagine and spoon half of the tomato and pepper mixture over them. Place the chunks of marinated fish on top and spoon the rest of the tomato and pepper mixture over the fish. Tuck the olives in and around the fish and drizzle the remaining tablespoon of olive oil over the top. Pour in roughly 125 ml/½ cup water and check the seasoning. Cover with a lid and steam for 15–20 minutes, until the fish is cooked through. Serve immediately with wedges of lemon.

Creamy shellfish tagine with fennel and harissa

In some coastal areas of Morocco, such as Casablanca and Tangier, restaurants offer shellfish tagines – a modern speciality, rather than a traditional one. Whether these dishes are the result of colonial French influence or simply devised for the tourists, they are certainly very tasty. They are best appreciated on their own, with chunks of crusty bread to mop up the creamy sauce.

500 g/1 lb. 2 oz. fresh mussels in their shells, scrubbed clean and rinsed

500 g/1 lb. 2 oz. fresh prawns/shrimp in their shells, thoroughly rinsed

freshly squeezed juice of 1 lemon

2 tablespoons olive oil

4–6 shallots, finely chopped

1 fennel bulb, chopped

1–2 teaspoons harissa (see page 8)

150 ml/¾ cup double/heavy cream

sea salt and freshly ground black pepper

a generous bunch of fresh coriander/cilantro, finely chopped

SERVES 4–6

Put the mussels and prawns/shrimp in a wide saucepan with just enough water to cover them. Add the lemon juice, cover the pan and bring the liquid to the boil. Shake the pan and cook the shellfish for about 3 minutes, until the shells of the mussels have opened. Drain the shellfish, reserve the liquor, and discard any mussels that have not opened. Refresh the mussels and prawns/shrimp under cold running water and shell most of them (you can, of course, leave them all in their shells if you prefer, as long as you are prepared for messy eating).

Heat the olive oil in a tagine or a heavy-based casserole. Stir in the shallots and fennel and sauté until soft. Stir in the harissa and pour in 300 ml/1¼ cups of the reserved cooking liquor. Bring the liquid to the boil and continue to boil for 2–3 minutes, reduce the heat and stir in the cream.

Simmer gently for about 5 minutes to let the flavours mingle, season to taste with salt and lots of black pepper, and stir in the mussels and prawns/shrimp. Toss in half the coriander/cilantro, cover with a lid and cook gently for about 5 minutes. Sprinkle the remaining coriander/cilantro over the top and serve immediately.

Fish tagine with preserved lemon and mint

900 g/2 lb. fresh fish fillets, such as cod or haddock, cut into large chunks

2–3 tablespoons olive oil

1 red onion, finely chopped

2 carrots, finely chopped

2 celery sticks, finely chopped

1 preserved lemon (see page 13), finely chopped

1 x 400-g/14-oz can of plum tomatoes with their juice

150 ml/⅔ cup fish stock or water

150 ml/⅔ cup white wine or fino sherry

sea salt and freshly ground black pepper

a bunch of fresh mint leaves, finely shredded

For the chermoula

2–3 garlic cloves, chopped

1 red chilli/chile, deseeded and chopped

1 teaspoon sea salt

a small bunch of fresh coriander/cilantro

a pinch of saffron threads

1–2 teaspoons ground cumin

3–4 tablespoons olive oil

freshly squeezed juice of 1 lemon

SERVES 4

The fish tagines of coastal Morocco are often made with whole fish, or with large chunks of fleshy fish such as sea bass, monkfish and cod. The fish is first marinated in the classic chermoula flavouring, and the dish is given an additional fillip with a little white wine or sherry. Serve with new potatoes and a leafy salad.

First, make the chermoula. Using a mortar and pestle, pound the garlic and chilli/chile with the salt to form a paste. Add the coriander/cilantro leaves and pound to a coarse paste. Beat in the saffron threads and cumin and bind well with the olive oil and lemon juice (you can whizz all the ingredients together in an electric blender, if you prefer). Reserve 2 teaspoons of the mixture for cooking. Toss the fish chunks in the remaining chermoula, cover and leave to marinate in the refrigerator for 1–2 hours.

Heat the oil in a tagine or a heavy-based casserole. Stir in the onion, carrots and celery and sauté until softened. Add the preserved lemon (reserving a little for sprinkling) with the reserved 2 teaspoons of chermoula and the tomatoes and stir in well. Cook gently for about 10 minutes to reduce the liquid, then add the stock and the wine or sherry. Bring the liquid to the boil, cover the tagine, reduce the heat and simmer for 10–15 minutes.

Toss the fish chunks in the tagine, cover and cook gently for 6–8 minutes, until the fish is cooked through. Season to taste with salt and pepper, sprinkle with the reserved preserved lemon and the shredded mint leaves and serve immediately.

beans & pulses

Roasted aubergine, tomato and chickpea tagine with yogurt

This delicious tagine has unmistakable Middle Eastern and Turkish notes influenced by the nation's history of invasion. Served with toasted flatbreads and a salad, this tagine is both warming and nourishing.

2–3 tablespoons ghee or smen (see page 12), or 1 tablespoon olive oil plus 1 tablespoon butter

2 teaspoons cumin seeds

2–3 cinnamon sticks

2 aubergines/eggplants, diced

2–3 garlic cloves, crushed

1–2 dried red chillies/chiles, finely chopped

8–10 cherry or baby plum tomatoes, halved

1–2 teaspoons sugar

2 teaspoons dried thyme

a 400-g/14-oz. can of chickpeas, drained and rinsed

1 preserved lemon (see page 13), finely chopped

2–3 tablespoons thick, creamy yogurt

freshly squeezed juice of ½ lemon

sea salt and freshly ground black pepper

dried mint, to garnish

SERVES 4

Preheat the oven to 200°C (400°F) Gas 6.

Heat the ghee in the base of a tagine or in a heavy-based casserole, stir in the cumin seeds and cinnamon sticks and sauté for 1–2 minutes. Toss in the aubergines/eggplants, cover and transfer the tagine to the preheated oven. Roast for 25–30 minutes, turning the aubergines/eggplants once or twice in the ghee and spices during cooking, until tender and golden brown.

Remove the tagine from the oven and toss in the garlic, chilli/chile and tomatoes. Sprinkle the sugar over the top, then return the tagine to the oven for a further 15 minutes. Remove from the oven again, toss in the thyme, chickpeas and preserved lemon, and season well with salt and pepper. Return the tagine to the oven for 10 minutes.

In a bowl, beat together the yogurt and lemon juice. Drizzle the yogurt over the tagine, then sprinkle a little dried mint over the top to garnish before serving.

Artichoke tagine with broad beans, apricots and almonds

Light and cheerful, this is a lovely tagine to make in the spring or early summer when the globe artichokes are young and tender. You can use fresh artichokes, trimmed to their bottoms, or the frozen ready-prepared bottoms available in some supermarkets. Serve with couscous or a salad.

4 artichoke bottoms

125 ml/½ cup olive oil

freshly squeezed juice of 1 lemon

150 g/1 cup blanched almonds

150 g/1 cup ready-to-eat dried apricots, halved or quartered

a 400-g/14-oz. can of broad/fava or butter beans, drained and rinsed

1–2 teaspoons sugar

a small bunch of fresh dill, roughly chopped

sea salt and freshly ground black pepper

SERVES 4

Put the artichoke bottoms, hollow-side up, in the base of a tagine or in a heavy-based saucepan.

Mix together the olive oil, lemon juice and 50 ml/ 3 tablespoons water and pour it over the artichokes. Put the lid on the tagine and cook the artichokes for 15–20 minutes over gentle heat, until tender.

Add the almonds, apricots and beans to the tagine. Sprinkle the sugar over them and scatter some of the dill over the top. Put the lid back on and cook gently for a further 10 minutes.

Season the tagine with salt and pepper. Spoon the almonds, apricots and beans into the middle of each artichoke bottom, garnish with the rest of the dill, and serve.

Butter bean tagine with cherry tomatoes and black olives

200 g/1⅓ cups dried butter beans, soaked overnight in plenty of water

2–3 tablespoons olive oil

4 garlic cloves, halved and smashed

2 onions, sliced

2 green chillies/chiles, deseeded and finely sliced

a thumb-sized piece of fresh ginger, peeled and finely chopped

2 teaspoons coriander seeds

1–2 teaspoons sugar

a pinch of saffron threads, soaked in a little water

about 12 cherry tomatoes

about 12 black olives, pitted

1–2 teaspoons dried thyme

freshly squeezed juice of 1 lemon

sea salt and freshly ground black pepper

a small bunch of fresh flat-leaf parsley, roughly chopped, to garnish

lemon wedges, to serve

SERVES 4–6

This is a delightfully sophisticated tagine, probably a legacy of the French, as it manages to combine three main ingredients with the essential Moroccan flavours of salty, fruity and fiery. You can serve this tagine as a side dish or as a main dish with a leafy salad.

Drain and rinse the soaked beans. Put them in a deep pan with plenty of water and bring it to the boil for about 5 minutes. Reduce the heat and simmer gently for about an hour, or until the beans are tender but not mushy. Drain and refresh the beans under running cold water.

Heat the oil in the base of a tagine or in a heavy-based saucepan. Add the garlic, onions, chillies/chiles, ginger, coriander seeds and sugar and sauté for 2–3 minutes. Stir in the saffron, along with its soaking water, and toss in the beans. Add the tomatoes, olives, dried thyme and lemon juice, cover with the lid and cook over a gentle heat for 15–20 minutes.

Season the tagine with salt and pepper, garnish with the parsley and serve with wedges of lemon to squeeze over the tagine.

Chickpea and spinach tagine with yogurt

1 tablespoon ghee, smen (see page 12) or argan oil, or 1 tablespoon olive oil plus 1 tablespoon butter

1 onion, finely chopped

2 garlic cloves, finely chopped

a thumb-sized piece of fresh ginger, peeled and finely chopped

1 teaspoon cumin seeds

250 g/1⅔ cups cooked chickpeas

1 teaspoon ground turmeric

1–2 teaspoons ras el hanout (see page 11)

500 g/1 lb. 2 oz. spinach, steamed and roughly chopped

2–3 tablespoons thick, creamy yogurt

½ teaspoon paprika

sea salt and freshly ground black pepper

SERVES 3–4

This village tagine is usually served with freshly griddled flatbreads, or a warm crusty loaf. If you use canned chickpeas and steam the spinach ahead of time, the tagine takes only 15–20 minutes – ideal for a quick lunch or supper.

Heat the ghee in the base of a tagine or in a heavy-based saucepan, add the onion, garlic, ginger and cumin seeds and sauté until they begin to colour. Toss in the chickpeas, coating them in the onion mixture, and stir in the ground turmeric and ras el hanout. Add the spinach and 150 ml/⅔ cup water. Put the lid on the tagine and cook over gentle heat for 10–15 minutes.

Season the tagine with salt and pepper, swirl in the yogurt, dust with the paprika and serve immediately.

Cauliflower and chickpea tagine with harissa and preserved lemon

This hearty tagine is typical of the type of dish cooked in the wooded Middle Atlas region and the lush valleys leading up to the High Atlas. It's a tasty way of preparing cauliflower, broccoli or cabbage, and is often simply served with chunks of bread to mop up the sauce.

2 tablespoons ghee, smen (see page 12) or argan oil, or 1 tablespoon olive oil plus 1 tablespoon butter

1 onion, coarsely chopped

2 garlic cloves, coarsely chopped

2 teaspoons coriander seeds

1–2 teaspoons sugar

a 400-g/14-oz. can of chickpeas, rinsed and drained

1 cauliflower, trimmed into small florets

a 400-g/14-oz. can of chopped tomatoes

2–3 teaspoons harissa (see page 8)

a bunch of fresh coriander/cilantro, roughly chopped

1 preserved lemon (see page 13), finely chopped

sea salt and freshly ground black pepper

SERVES 4–6

Heat the ghee in the base of a tagine or in a heavy-based saucepan, add the onion and sauté for 2–3 minutes to soften. Add the garlic, coriander seeds and sugar and cook for a further 2–3 minutes, until the onion and garlic begin to colour, then toss in the chickpeas and cauliflower florets.

Add the chopped tomatoes, stir in the harissa and pour in just enough water to cover the cauliflower. Bring the liquid to the boil, reduce the heat, put on the lid, and cook the tagine gently for about 20 minutes, until the cauliflower is tender.

Season the tagine well with salt and pepper, toss in half the coriander/cilantro and preserved lemon, and cook for a further 5–10 minutes.

Garnish with the remaining coriander/cilantro and preserved lemon and serve.

Bean tagine with harissa and coriander

This is a classic Berber tagine, which can be found in infinite variations throughout Morocco using different beans – haricot, borlotti, black-eyed, broad/fava or butter beans. Often this dish is served on its own with chunks of bread, but it is also delicious served with thick, creamy yogurt and a Moroccan fruit chutney.

450 g/1 lb. dried haricot beans, soaked overnight and drained

2–3 tablespoons ghee, smen (see page 12) or argan oil, or 1 tablespoon olive oil plus 1 tablespoon butter

2 onions, finely chopped

4 garlic cloves, finely chopped

2 red chillies/chiles, deseeded and finely chopped

2 teaspoons sugar

2 teaspoons harissa (see page 8)

2 x 400-g/14-oz. cans of chopped tomatoes

a bunch of fresh mint leaves, finely chopped

a bunch of fresh flat-leaf parsley, finely chopped

a bunch of fresh coriander/ cilantro, finely chopped

sea salt and freshly ground black pepper

1–2 lemons, cut into wedges, to serve

SERVES 4–6

Put the beans in a saucepan with plenty of water and bring to the boil. Reduce the heat and simmer for about 30 minutes until the beans are tender. Drain thoroughly.

Heat the ghee in the base of a tagine or in a heavy-based saucepan, add the onions, garlic, chillies/chiles and sugar and sauté for 2–3 minutes, until they begin to colour. Stir in the harissa and toss in the drained beans. Add the tomatoes and top up with a little water to make sure the beans are submerged. Bring the liquid to the boil, reduce the heat, put on the lid and cook gently for about 30 minutes.

Season the tagine with salt and pepper to taste, stir in most of the herbs and simmer for a further 10 minutes. Garnish with the remaining herbs and serve hot with the wedges of lemon to squeeze over the tagine.

Lentil tagine with ginger and ras el hanout

Packed with flavour, this spicy lentil tagine is best served on its own with a dollop of thick, creamy yogurt, a Moroccan fruit chutney and toasted flatbread. From the chill air of the Atlas Mountains, this tagine is designed to warm you from within.

2 tablespoons ghee or smen (see page 12), or 1 tablespoon olive oil plus 1 tablespoon butter

1 onion, finely chopped

a large thumb-sized piece of fresh ginger, peeled and finely chopped

4 garlic cloves, finely chopped

1–2 teaspoons sugar

2 teaspoons cumin seeds

1 teaspoon coriander seeds

2–3 teaspoons ras el hanout (see page 11)

300 g/1½ cups brown lentils, rinsed and drained

a large bunch of fresh coriander/cilantro, finely chopped

sea salt and freshly ground black pepper

SERVES 4–6

Heat the ghee in the base of a tagine or in a heavy-based saucepan, stir in the onion, ginger, garlic and sugar and sauté for 2–3 minutes until they soften and begin to colour. Add the cumin and coriander seeds and cook for a further 1–2 minutes, then stir in the ras el hanout and toss in the lentils, making sure they are thoroughly coated.

Pour in enough water to cover the lentils by about 2.5 cm/ 1 inch and bring it to the boil. Reduce the heat, put on the lid and simmer gently for about 35 minutes, until all the liquid has been absorbed but the lentils still have a bite to them.

Season the lentils with salt and pepper to taste, toss in most of the coriander/cilantro and garnish with the rest.

Spicy carrot and chickpea tagine with turmeric and coriander

Chickpeas and other pulses often feature in the tagines of arid areas and poorer communities as they provide protein and nourishment where meat is scarce. Combined with vegetables and spices, hearty tagines like this one are also popular in the street stalls and cafés of Fes and Marrakesh.

2 tablespoons ghee or smen (see page 12), or 1 tablespoon olive oil plus 1 tablespoon butter

1 large onion, finely chopped

1–2 red chillies/chiles, deseeded and finely chopped

2–3 garlic cloves, finely chopped

2 teaspoons cumin seeds

2 teaspoons coriander seeds

1–2 teaspoons sugar

2–3 carrots, peeled, halved lengthways and thickly sliced

2 x 400-g/14-oz. cans of chickpeas, thoroughly rinsed and drained

2 teaspoons ground turmeric

1 teaspoon ground cinnamon

a bunch of fresh coriander/ cilantro, leaves finely chopped

sea salt and freshly ground black pepper

SERVES 4

Heat the ghee in the base of a tagine or in a heavy-based saucepan, stir in the onion, chillies/chiles, garlic, cumin and coriander seeds and the sugar and sauté for 2–3 minutes, until the onion begins to colour. Toss in the carrots and cook for a further 1–2 minutes, then add the chickpeas.

Stir in the turmeric and cinnamon and pour in enough water to cover the base of the tagine. Bring the water to the boil, put on the lid, and cook over a gentle heat for 20–25 minutes, topping up the water if necessary, until the carrots are tender.

Season the tagine with salt and pepper, stir in most of the coriander/cilantro, and garnish with the remainder.

vegetables

Three pepper tagine with eggs and ras el hanout

This is one of the typical street tagines served up at market stalls, bus stations, busy ports and working men's cafés. Quick and cheerful, it can be prepared for a snack at any time of day, or for a light meal with toasted flatbreads and garlic-flavoured yogurt.

2 tablespoons ghee or olive oil

1 onion, halved lengthways and sliced

1 teaspoon cumin seeds

1 teaspoon sugar

3 (bell) peppers (green, red and yellow), deseeded and sliced

1–2 teaspoons ras el hanout (see page 11), plus a little extra for sprinkling

4 eggs

4 generous tablespoons thick, creamy yogurt

2 garlic cloves, crushed

sea salt and freshly ground black pepper

a small bunch of fresh flat-leaf parsley, finely chopped, to garnish

SERVES 4

Heat the ghee in the base of a tagine or in a heavy-based saucepan, stir in the onion, cumin seeds and sugar and sauté for 1–2 minutes. Add the peppers and cook over a medium heat for a further 2–3 minutes, until they have softened. Stir in the ras el hanout and season with salt and pepper.

Push the peppers to the sides of the tagine to make room for the eggs. Crack the eggs into the middle of the tagine and dust them with a little ras el hanout. Put the lid on the tagine and cook the eggs over gentle heat for 3–4 minutes, until the whites are just firm.

In a mixing bowl, beat the yogurt with the garlic until smooth and season it with salt and pepper to taste. Garnish the tagine with the parsley, divide the eggs and peppers onto 4 plates, and serve with a spoonful of the garlic-flavoured yogurt.

Roasted cherry tomato tagine with feta and preserved lemon

Simple and tasty, this tagine offers a great way of cooking cherry or baby plum tomatoes. It can be served as a snack with flatbreads or chunks of crusty bread, or as an accompaniment to grilled and roasted dishes. It is also delicious without the feta, so vegans can enjoy this dish too.

450 g/1 lb. cherry tomatoes

2 tablespoons olive or argan oil

4 garlic cloves, halved and smashed

1 teaspoon sugar

1–2 teaspoons finely chopped dried or fresh chillies/chiles

1–2 teaspoons dried oregano

1 preserved lemon (see page 13), finely chopped

sea salt

120 g/4 oz. feta cheese

SERVES 4

Preheat the oven to 200°C (400°F) Gas 6.

Tip the cherry tomatoes into the base of a tagine or into a heavy-based casserole and drizzle with the oil. Scatter the smashed garlic around the tomatoes, then sprinkle the sugar, chillies/chiles and nearly all of the oregano over the top. Give the tagine a good shake, then place it in the preheated oven for 20–25 minutes, until the tomato skins begin to buckle.

Remove the tagine from the oven and toss in half of the preserved lemon. Season with salt, sprinkle the rest of the oregano over the top and pop the tagine back in the oven for 5–10 minutes.

Crumble the feta over the top and garnish with the remaining preserved lemon before serving.

Spicy roasted pumpkin tagine with lime

This is a tasty way of enjoying pumpkin. These spicy wedges can be served as an accompaniment to other tagines, or on their own with a spicy couscous and a salad. Save the seeds and roast them lightly with a little oil and coarse salt to serve as a quick snack.

1 small or ½ medium-sized pumpkin

2 teaspoons coriander seeds

1 teaspoon cumin seeds

1 teaspoon fennel seeds

1–2 teaspoons ground cinnamon

2 dried red chillies/chiles, finely chopped

1 teaspoon sea salt

2 garlic cloves, crushed

2–3 tablespoons olive or pumpkin seed oil

1–2 tablespoons honey

1–2 limes, cut into wedges, to serve

SERVES 4–6

Preheat the oven to 200°C (400°F) Gas 6.

Cut the pumpkin in half lengthways and scoop out the seeds with a spoon. Slice each pumpkin half into 4–6 thin wedges, like crescent moons, and arrange them, skin-side down, in a circle in the base of a wide tagine or in a heavy-based casserole.

Using a mortar and pestle, grind all the dried spices with the salt. Add the garlic and enough oil to form a paste. Rub the spicy paste over the pumpkin wedges and drizzle the rest of the oil over them.

Pop the tagine in the preheated oven and roast the pumpkin wedges for 35–40 minutes, until tender. Drizzle the honey over the wedges and return to the oven for a further 10 minutes. Sprinkle a little salt over the pumpkin wedges and serve hot with the lime to squeeze over them.

Baby aubergine tagine with coriander and mint

This is a tasty way of cooking the baby aubergines/eggplants that are often available in Middle Eastern, North African and Asian stores. However, if you can't find them, you can use the slender aubergines/eggplants cut into quarters. Serve this dish with Plain Buttery Couscous (see page 120).

2 tablespoons ghee, or argan or olive oil

1 onion, finely chopped

2–3 garlic cloves, finely chopped

2 red chillies/chile, deseeded and finely chopped

2 teaspoons coriander seeds

2 teaspoons cumin seeds

2 teaspoons sugar

1–2 teaspoons ground fenugreek

8 baby aubergines/eggplants, with stalks intact

2 x 400-g/14-oz. cans of chopped tomatoes

a bunch of fresh mint leaves, roughly chopped

a bunch of fresh coriander/ cilantro, roughly chopped

sea salt and freshly ground black pepper

SERVES 4

Heat the ghee in the base of a tagine or in a heavy-based saucepan. Stir in the onion, garlic, chillies/chiles, coriander and cumin seeds and sugar and sauté for 2–3 minutes, until the onion begins to colour.

Toss in the fenugreek and the aubergines/eggplants, rolling them in the onion and spice mixture. Tip in the tomatoes, bubble them up, put on the tagine lid and cook over a gentle heat for about 40 minutes, until the baby aubergines/ eggplants are very tender.

Season the tagine with salt and pepper and toss in most of the mint and coriander/cilantro. Put the lid back on and cook over a medium heat for a further 5 minutes. Garnish with the rest of the mint and coriander/cilantro and serve hot.

Baby courgette tagine with courgette flowers and lemon

A unique spring and early summer dish, this tagine is made with baby courgettes/zucchini and the lovely bright yellow flowers of the plant. It is light and lemony and can be served as a first course, as a salad, or as a simple tagine with a little bit of fresh crusty bread to mop up the juices.

2 tablespoons olive or argan oil

2 teaspoons coriander seeds

2 garlic cloves, finely chopped

1 onion, finely chopped

12 baby courgettes/zucchini, trimmed and left whole

1 preserved lemon (see page 13), finely sliced

freshly squeezed juice of 2 lemons

4–8 courgette/zucchini flowers, trimmed and left whole

1 tablespoon orange blossom water

sea salt and freshly ground black pepper

a few fresh mint leaves, finely shredded, to garnish

SERVES 4

Heat the oil in the base of a tagine or in a heavy-based saucepan, stir in the coriander seeds, garlic and onion and sauté for 1–2 minutes. Toss in the baby courgettes/zucchini, coating them in the onion and garlic, then add the preserved lemon and lemon juice. Put the lid on the tagine and cook gently for 10–15 minutes, until the courgettes/zucchini are tender but still have a bite to them.

Season the tagine with salt and pepper, toss in the courgette/zucchini flowers and splash in the orange blossom water. Put the lid back on and cook gently for 4–5 minutes, until the flowers have wilted in the steam.

Garnish with the shredded mint leaves and serve hot, or at room temperature.

Okra and tomato tagine with lemon

It is important to know how to prepare okra before cooking so that they retain their colour and bite, otherwise they can become quite mushy and gelatinous. First, the okra need to be trimmed by cutting off the stalks; then place them in a bowl and toss them well in 2–3 teaspoons salt and 2–3 tablespoons white wine or cider vinegar. Leave the okra to sit for at least 2 hours, then rinse, drain and pat them dry before using. Serve this tagine with plain or spicy couscous.

2 tablespoons olive or argan oil

1 onion, halved lengthways and finely sliced

2 garlic cloves, finely chopped

1–2 red chillies/chiles, deseeded and finely chopped

1–2 teaspoons sugar

2 teaspoons coriander seeds

500 g/1 lb. 2 oz. fresh okra, rinsed and prepared as above

freshly squeezed juice of 1 lemon

a 400-g/14-oz. can of chopped tomatoes

sea salt and freshly ground black pepper

½ preserved lemon (see page 13), finely sliced, to garnish

SERVES 4

Heat the oil in the base of a tagine or in a heavy-based saucepan. Stir in the onion, garlic, chilli/chile, sugar and coriander seeds and sauté for 2–3 minutes. Toss in the okra and add the lemon juice. Tip in the tomatoes, bubble them up, put the lid on the tagine and cook over a medium heat for 15 minutes, until the okra is tender.

Season the tagine with salt and pepper, garnish with the preserved lemon, and serve.

Runner bean tagine with tomato and dill

This simple fresh bean tagine is best enjoyed on its own with chunks of fresh crusty bread and thick, creamy yogurt. Be quite liberal with the dill as it is the only flavouring in the tagine and transforms a traditional bean and tomato dish into something deliciously unique.

2 tablespoons olive or argan oil

1–2 onions, roughly chopped

2 garlic cloves, roughly chopped

500 g/1 lb. 2 oz. fresh runner/stringless beans, trimmed and cut into 3 or 4 pieces

2 teaspoons sugar

freshly squeezed juice of 1 lemon

2 x 400-g/14-oz. cans of chopped tomatoes

a bunch of fresh dill, roughly chopped

sea salt and freshly ground black pepper

a small bunch of fresh flat-leaf parsley, roughly chopped, to garnish

SERVES 4–6

Heat the oil in the base of a tagine or in a heavy-based saucepan, stir in the onions and garlic and sauté for 2–3 minutes, until the onions soften. Toss in the beans, coating them in the onions and oil, then stir in the sugar and lemon juice. Add the tomatoes and dill, cover with the lid and cook over gentle heat for about 40 minutes, until the beans are tender and the tomato sauce is fairly thick.

Season the tagine with salt and pepper and garnish with the parsley before serving.

Artichokes with ginger, honey and preserved lemon

For this recipe, you can use fresh globe artichokes, preserved artichoke hearts or frozen artichoke bottoms. To prepare fresh globe artichokes, first remove the outer leaves and cut off the stems. Then, using a teaspoon, scoop out the choke and all the hairy bits. Trim the hearts and bottoms and immerse them in water mixed with a squeeze of lemon juice to prevent them from blackening. Serve the tagine with a lemon, spicy or fruity couscous.

2 tablespoons olive oil

2 garlic cloves, crushed

1 thumb-sized piece of fresh ginger, peeled and finely chopped

1 teaspoon fennel seeds

a pinch of saffron threads, soaked in a little water

freshly squeezed juice of ½ lemon

1–2 tablespoons honey

6–8 artichoke hearts, halved, or artichoke bottoms, cut into quarters

1 preserved lemon (see page 13), finely sliced

a small bunch of fresh coriander/cilantro, finely chopped

sea salt and freshly ground black pepper

SERVES 4

Heat the oil in the base of a tagine or in a heavy-based saucepan, stir in the garlic, ginger and fennel seeds and sauté for 1–2 minutes. Add the saffron, along with its soaking water, lemon juice and honey and simmer gently over a low heat.

Drain the artichokes and add them to the tagine, tossing them in the spices and honey. Add just enough water (roughly 150 ml/⅔ cup) to cover the base of the tagine and stir in most of the preserved lemon. Put the lid on the tagine and cook gently for about 15–20 minutes, until the artichokes are tender.

Season the tagine with salt and pepper and toss in most of the coriander/cilantro. Garnish with the rest of the preserved lemon and coriander/cilantro to serve.

Carrot and potato tagine with peas

This is a classic peasant or 'poor man's' tagine, which can be easily adapted to suit the season or the budget by substituting the peas with beans, chickpeas or chopped turnip or cabbage. Serve with plain couscous, rice or chunks of crusty bread.

1 tablespoon butter or ghee

2 onions, halved and sliced with the grain

4 garlic cloves, chopped

a thumb-sized piece of fresh ginger, peeled and chopped

1–2 red chillies/chiles, deseeded and finely chopped

1 teaspoon cumin seeds

1 teaspoon coriander seeds

2 teaspoons ground turmeric

8 small potatoes, peeled and left whole

3–4 carrots, peeled and cut into 3–4 chunks

600 ml/2½ cups vegetable stock

225 g/1½ cups freshly shelled or frozen peas

a small bunch of fresh flat-leaf parsley, finely chopped

a small bunch of fresh mint, finely chopped

sea salt and freshly ground black pepper

SERVES 4

Heat the butter or ghee in the base of a tagine or in a heavy-based saucepan, stir in the onions, garlic, ginger, chillies/chiles and the cumin and coriander seeds and sauté for 2–3 minutes. Add the turmeric and the potatoes and carrots. Pour in the stock and bring it to the boil. Put the lid on the tagine, reduce the heat and cook gently for 15–20 minutes, until the potatoes and carrots are tender.

Toss in the peas, add half the parsley and mint, and season with salt and pepper. Add a little extra water, if necessary, put the lid back on and cook gently for 5–6 minutes. Garnish with the rest of the parsley and mint before serving.

Roasted potato, onion and fennel tagine with sumac and balsamic vinegar

Potatoes often feature in peasant or 'poor man's' tagines with onions and garlic and perhaps a few herbs or spices. This roasted variation of a classic poor man's tagine is delicious served with a fresh tomato or fruit-based salad.

500 g/1 lb. 2 oz. new potatoes, unpeeled

2 tablespoons ghee, smen (see page 12) or argan oil, or 1 tablespoon olive oil plus 1 tablespoon butter

2 onions, halved lengthways and sliced with the grain

2 fennel bulbs, trimmed and finely sliced in their skins (reserve the fronds to garnish)

4–6 garlic cloves, smashed in their skins

2–3 tablespoons balsamic vinegar

1–2 teaspoons sumac

a small bunch of fresh flat-leaf parsley, roughly chopped

sea salt and freshly ground black pepper

SERVES 4

Preheat oven to 200°C (400°F) Gas 6.

Put the potatoes in a large saucepan and top up with enough water to cover them. Bring the water to the boil and cook the potatoes for 5–6 minutes. Drain, refresh them under cold water, then thickly slice.

Heat the ghee in the base of a tagine or in a heavy-based casserole, stir in the onions and sauté for 3–4 minutes, until they begin to soften and colour. Stir in the fennel and garlic cloves and cook for a further 2–3 minutes. Toss in the potatoes and season with salt and pepper.

Put the tagine in the preheated oven, uncovered, and cook for 35–40 minutes, until the potatoes are golden and slightly roasted.

Toss in the balsamic vinegar and sprinkle the sumac, parsley and fennel fronds over the tagine to serve.

Sweet potato tagine with green olives and orange blossom water

Sweet potatoes and yams are popular in village tagines as they work well with spices, dried fruits and tangy flavourings and they tend to fill the stomach quite quickly. This unusual tagine from Casablanca is a more sophisticated version with the floral notes of orange blossom water and can be served hot in the winter, or at room temperature in the summer with wedges of lemon to squeeze over it. A spicy couscous dish makes the perfect accompaniment.

2–3 tablespoons olive or argan oil

1 onion, roughly chopped

1 teaspoon cumin seeds

a thumb-sized piece of fresh ginger, peeled and finely chopped

2–3 sweet potatoes, peeled and cut into bite-sized chunks

½ teaspoon smoked paprika

8–12 cracked green olives, rinsed and drained

1 preserved lemon (see page 13), finely chopped

freshly squeezed juice of ½ lemon

3–4 tablespoons orange blossom water

sea salt and freshly ground black pepper

a small bunch of fresh coriander/ cilantro, to garnish

SERVES 4–6

Heat the olive oil in the base of a tagine or in a heavy-based saucepan, stir in the onion and sauté for 2–3 minutes, until it begins to soften and colour. Add the cumin seeds and ginger and cook until fragrant. Toss in the sweet potatoes along with the paprika and pour in just enough water to just cover the base of the tagine. Put on the lid and cook gently for 10–15 minutes, until the sweet potato is tender, but firm, and the liquid has reduced.

Toss in the olives, preserved lemon, lemon juice and orange blossom water. Replace the lid and cook gently for a further 10 minutes. Season the tagine with salt and pepper to taste, garnish with the coriander/cilantro and serve.

Baked vegetable tagine with preserved lemon

3–4 tablespoons olive or argan oil

2 onions, halved and sliced with the grain

4 garlic cloves, finely chopped

a large thumb-sized piece of fresh ginger, peeled and finely chopped

2 red chillies/chiles, deseeded and finely chopped

2 teaspoons cumin seeds

2 teaspoons coriander seeds

1–2 teaspoons sugar

4 potatoes, peeled and thickly sliced

2 carrots, peeled and thickly sliced

1 small cabbage, trimmed and cut into thick slices

about 600 ml/2½ cups vegetable stock

225 g/1½ cups freshly shelled or frozen peas

1 preserved lemon (see page 13), finely sliced

a bunch of fresh mint, finely shredded

a bunch of fresh coriander/cilantro, finely chopped

6 large tomatoes, finely sliced

1 tablespoon butter, cut into little pieces

sea salt and freshly ground black pepper

SERVES 4–6

Oven-cooked tagines are either roasted in the open tagine base, or they are baked in traditional Berber tagines, which have a flatter domed lid compared with the classic, steep conical one. This oven-baked Berber recipe for seasonal vegetables is a delicious way of celebrating the harvest, served hot with a mound of Plain Buttery Couscous (see page 120).

Preheat oven to 180°C (350°F) Gas 4.

Heat the oil in the base of a tagine or in a heavy-based saucepan, stir in the onions and sauté for 2 minutes to soften them a little. Stir in the garlic, ginger, chillies/chiles, cumin and coriander seeds, and the sugar and cook for a further 1–2 minutes, until the onions begin to colour.

Toss in the potatoes and carrots and cook for 1–2 minutes, then stir in the cabbage. Pour in the stock, making sure it almost covers the vegetables, and bring it to the boil. Put the lid on the tagine and put it in the preheated oven for about 30 minutes.

Add all of the peas and most of the preserved lemon, mint and coriander/cilantro to the tagine, and season with salt and pepper. Arrange the tomato slices, overlapping each other, on top of the vegetables and scatter the butter over the tomatoes. Return the tagine, without the lid, to the oven for about 15 minutes more, until the tomatoes are lightly browned.

Garnish the tagine with the rest of the preserved lemon, mint and coriander/cilantro, and serve.

Roasted sweet potato tagine with ginger, cinnamon and honey

This is a very tasty way of cooking potatoes, ideal as an accompaniment for numerous grilled and roasted dishes, or simply on its own with garlic-flavoured yogurt and chunks of crusty bread.

2 tablespoons ghee, or
  1 tablespoon olive oil plus
  1 tablespoon butter

a large thumb-sized piece of fresh
  ginger, peeled and cut into
  very thin sticks

4 garlic cloves, peeled and cut
  into thin sticks

4–6 cinnamon sticks

4–6 sweet potatoes, peeled and
  cut into bite-sized chunks

1–2 tablespoons runny honey

sea salt and freshly ground
  black pepper

a small bunch of fresh coriander/
  cilantro, finely chopped,
  to garnish

For the yogurt

400 ml/1⅔ cups thick, creamy
  yogurt

1–2 garlic cloves, crushed

sea salt and freshly ground
  black pepper

SERVES 4–6

Preheat oven to 200°C (400°F) Gas 6.

Melt the ghee in the base of a tagine or in a heavy-based casserole, stir in the ginger, garlic and cinnamon sticks and sauté for 1 minute. Add the sweet potatoes and toss in the spices to coat, then pop the tagine, uncovered, in the preheated oven for 45 minutes.

Remove the tagine from the oven and toss the potatoes in the ghee and flavourings, season with salt and pepper and drizzle over the honey. Return the tagine to the oven for a further 10–15 minutes, until the sweet potato is tender and slightly caramelized.

In a small bowl, beat together the yogurt and crushed garlic, then season with salt and pepper.

Garnish the sweet potato with the coriander/cilantro and serve it with the garlic-flavoured yogurt.

fruits & nuts

Stuffed prune tagine with walnuts and rosewater

The Romans got as far as Morocco and left many signs of their existence, including the production of wine, which the colonizing French took to new heights. There are several good wines produced in Morocco and occasionally wine is used in cooking, particularly by creative chefs in the restaurants of Rabat and Casablanca. Serve the tagine on its own between courses, or with buttery couscous, crumbled feta and pickled chillies/chiles.

16 ready-to-eat dried stoned/
   pitted prunes

16 walnut halves

1–2 tablespoons ghee, or
   1 tablespoon olive oil plus
   1 tablespoon butter

2 cinnamon sticks

1 teaspoon cardamom seeds

3–4 cloves

pared peel of ½ orange

250 ml/1 cup red wine

1 tablespoon pomegranate syrup

1 tablespoon honey

1–2 tablespoons rosewater

sea salt and freshly ground
   black pepper

a small bunch of fresh flat-leaf
   parsley, roughly chopped,
   to garnish

SERVES 4

Find the opening in each pitted prune and stuff it with a walnut half.

Melt the ghee in the base of a tagine or in a heavy-based saucepan, add the cinnamon sticks, cardamom seeds, cloves and orange peel and sauté for a minute, until fragrant. Add the stuffed prunes to the tagine, turning them over in the spices and ghee, then pour in the red wine. Put the lid on the tagine and cook gently for 15 minutes.

Stir in the pomegranate syrup and honey. Season the tagine with salt and pepper, put the lid back on and cook gently for another 10 minutes, until the juices begin to caramelize.

Splash in the rosewater, garnish with the parsley, and serve.

Roasted pear tagine with figs, walnuts and cardamom

Sweet, fruity and spicy – this unusual tagine has the hallmarks of an early Arab, or Persian, dish. It is delicious served alongside other tagines and with spicy couscous, or it can be served as a course on its own to balance the palate between spicy dishes.

1–2 tablespoons ghee or argan oil, or 1 tablespoon olive oil plus 1 tablespoon butter

1–2 teaspoons cardamom seeds

4 small pears, peeled, cored and cut into quarters

8–12 ready-to-eat dried figs, halved

175 g/1 generous cup walnut halves

1 dried red chilli/chile, finely chopped

2 tablespoons honey

a small bunch of fresh coriander/cilantro leaves, finely chopped

sea salt and freshly ground black pepper

1 lemon or lime, cut into wedges, to serve

SERVES 4

Preheat the oven to 200°C (400°F) Gas 6.

Heat the ghee in the base of a tagine or in a heavy-based casserole, stir in the cardamom seeds and sauté for 1 minute. Add the pears and toss them to coat in the spices, then put the tagine in the preheated oven for 15 minutes, turning the pears once during cooking.

Take the tagine out of the oven and toss in the dried figs, walnuts and chilli/chile. Drizzle the honey over the pears and return the tagine to the oven for about 15 minutes, until the pears begin to caramelize.

Season the tagine with salt and pepper and toss in most of the coriander/cilantro. Garnish the tagine with the rest of the coriander/cilantro and serve with wedges of lemon or lime.

Aubergine and courgette tagine with apricots and dates

3–4 tablespoons olive oil

20 g/1½ tablespoons butter

1 onion, halved lengthways and sliced into half moons

2–3 garlic cloves, chopped

2 aubergines/eggplants, cut into bite-sized chunks

2 courgettes/zucchini, cut into bite-sized chunks

1 red (bell) pepper, halved, deseeded and sliced

150 g/1 cup ready-to-eat stoned/pitted dried dates, halved lengthways

150 g/1 cup ready-to-eat dried apricots, halved

2–3 teaspoons ras el hanout (see page 11)

2 teaspoons sugar

2 x 400-g/14-oz. cans of chopped tomatoes

a small bunch of fresh flat-leaf parsley, finely chopped

a small bunch of fresh coriander/cilantro, finely chopped

sea salt and freshly ground black pepper

SERVES 4–6

This delicious tagine is like a Moroccan 'ratatouille' with the additional burst of sweet and spicy flavours from the dried fruits and the ras el hanout. It is a lovely dish to serve on its own with chunks of fresh crusty bread and a dollop of yogurt, but you can also serve it with couscous.

Heat the oil with the butter in the base of a tagine or in a heavy-based saucepan, stir in the onion and garlic and sauté for 1–2 minutes to soften. Toss in the aubergines/eggplants and courgettes/zucchini and cook for a further 3–4 minutes, then add the pepper, dates, apricots, ras el hanout and sugar. Stir in the tomatoes with half the herbs and bring to the boil. Cover with the lid and cook over a medium heat for 30–40 minutes.

Season the tagine with salt and pepper, garnish with the remaining herbs and serve.

Yam and shallot tagine with garlic, prunes and orange

This syrupy tagine is delicious served as an accompaniment to other tagines, or on its own with chunks of crusty bread to mop up the sweet sauce. Serve it with a tangy, crunchy or leafy salad to balance the sweetness.

2 tablespoons ghee, smen (see page 12) or argan oil, or 1 tablespoon olive oil plus 1 tablespoon butter

a large thumb-sized piece of fresh ginger, peeled and finely chopped

2 cinnamon sticks

8–12 small, round shallots, peeled and left whole

8 garlic cloves, peeled and left whole

1 yam, peeled and cut into bite-sized chunks

300 ml/1¼ cups vegetable stock

8–12 ready-to-eat dried stoned/pitted prunes

2 tablespoons honey

grated zest and freshly squeezed juice of 1 orange

1 tablespoon orange blossom water

a small bunch of fresh mint leaves, finely chopped or shredded

sea salt and freshly ground black pepper

SERVES 4–6

Heat the ghee in the base of a tagine or in a heavy-based saucepan, stir in the ginger and cinnamon sticks and sauté for 1–2 minutes.

Toss in the shallots, rolling them over in the ginger and ghee until they begin to colour, then add the garlic cloves and yam and cook for a further 1–2 minutes.

Pour in the vegetable stock, making sure you have enough to cover the base of the tagine, and bring it to the boil. Put on the lid, reduce the heat and cook gently for 15 minutes. Toss in the prunes, honey, orange zest and juice, and the orange blossom water, put the lid back on and cook over a medium heat for a further 10 minutes.

Remove the lid and continue to cook over a medium heat, until the liquid reduces and begins to caramelize. Season the tagine with salt and pepper and stir in most of the mint. Serve the tagine garnished with the remaining mint.

Pumpkin, apple and sultana tagine with chermoula

Chermoula is often used as a marinade for fish in tagines and grilled dishes, but it is sometimes employed in vegetable dishes too, particularly in the coastal regions. The combination of pumpkin and apple with the tangy, spicy chermoula makes this an interesting accompaniment to plain grilled or roasted dishes, as well as plain couscous.

2 tablespoons olive or argan oil

700 g/1 lb. 9 oz. pumpkin, skinned, deseeded and cut into bite-sized chunks

2 crisp apples, peeled, cored and cut into segments or bite-sized chunks

2 tablespoons sultanas/golden raisins or raisins

1 teaspoon smoked paprika

1 quantity chermoula (see page 10)

sea salt and freshly ground black pepper

a small bunch of fresh mint leaves, finely shredded, to garnish

SERVES 4–6

Heat the oil in the base of a tagine or in a heavy-based saucepan, toss in the pumpkin and sauté for 1–2 minutes. Add the apple and sultanas/golden raisins and cook for a further 1–2 minutes, until the sultanas/golden raisins plump up. Sprinkle in the paprika, stir in the chermoula and pour in enough water to cover the base of the tagine. Bring the water to the boil, put on the lid and cook over a medium heat for 20–25 minutes, until the pumpkin is tender.

Season the tagine with salt and pepper, garnish with a little shredded mint, and serve.

Roasted butternut squash tagine with rosemary, almonds and apricots

This is a tagine for banquets or a celebration in the home. When prepared for large numbers, the butternut squash is laid out in baking pans but for a family meal, it can be prepared in the base of a wide tagine. You can serve the roasted squash as an accompaniment to other tagines, or on its own with a spicy couscous.

1 butternut squash

2–3 tablespoons olive, argan or pumpkin seed oil

2 garlic cloves, crushed

4 sprigs of fresh rosemary

2 tablespoons flaked/slivered almonds

1–2 balls of preserved stem ginger, finely chopped

6–8 ready-to-eat dried apricots, finely chopped

1–2 tablespoons honey

sea salt and freshly ground black pepper

SERVES 4

Preheat oven to 200°C (400°F) Gas 6.

Cut the butternut squash in half lengthways and scoop out the seeds with a spoon. Cut the halves in half lenthways again and put them, skin-side down, in the base of a tagine or in a heavy-based casserole. Rub the oil and garlic over the butternut flesh and thread the rosemary sprigs diagonally through the fleshiest part (if the flesh is too firm, push a thin skewer through first to form the opening). Season the squash with salt and pepper and place the tagine in the preheated oven for 30–35 minutes, until the flesh is tender.

Meanwhile, roast the almonds in a dry frying pan/skillet until they turn golden brown and emit a nutty aroma. In a small bowl, combine the roasted almonds with the stem ginger and apricots.

Take the tagine out of the oven and spoon some of the almond, ginger and apricot mixture into the hollow of each butternut squash slice, then scatter the rest around the dish. Drizzle the honey over the top and return the tagine to the oven for a further 10 minutes. Serve immediately.

Butternut squash tagine with shallots and sultanas

Variations of this sweet and spicy tagine are often served in the restaurants of Tangier, Casablanca, Rabat and Fes, where the influence of the French, the Moors and the Arabs is often evident in the dishes. Enjoy the flavours of this tagine with a lemon or herb couscous and a tangy salad.

2 tablespoons olive or argan oil

4 garlic cloves, peeled and smashed

2 teaspoons fennel seeds

8–12 shallots, peeled and left whole

2–3 tablespoons sultanas/golden raisins

1–2 teaspoons harissa (see page 8)

1 butternut squash, peeled, deseeded and cut into bite-sized chunks

2 tablespoons honey

2 tablespoons pomegranate syrup

a small bunch of fresh coriander/cilantro leaves, finely chopped

sea salt and freshly ground black pepper

1–2 tablespoons pomegranate seeds, to garnish

SERVES 4

Heat the oil in the base of a tagine or in a heavy-based saucepan, stir in the garlic and fennel seeds and sauté for 1–2 minutes, until fragrant. Add the shallots, rolling them around in the oil, and cook for a further 2 minutes. Toss in the sultanas/golden raisins and cook until they plump up, then stir in the harissa and the butternut squash.

Pour in enough water to just cover the base of the tagine and bring it to the boil. Put on the lid and cook the tagine over a medium heat for 15 minutes, until the butternut squash is tender. Stir in the honey and pomegranate syrup and cook over a medium heat for a further 10 minutes.

Season the tagine with salt and pepper, stir in most of the coriander/cilantro and garnish with the rest of the coriander/cilantro and the pomegranate seeds.

couscous & salads

Plain buttery couscous

To many a Moroccan, a mound of light, buttery couscous is perfection on a plate. After all the fluffing and aerating of the couscous, each grain should be separated and the dish should emit the sweet, warming aroma of melted butter. Go further and add almonds and cinnamon to the dish and what you have is, undoubtedly, the king of couscous dishes – the most popular and practical of all.

350 g/2 cups couscous

½ teaspoon sea salt

400 ml/1⅔ cups warm water

2 tablespoons sunflower or olive oil

25 g/2 tablespoons butter, cut into little pieces

For the top (optional)

15 g/1 tablespoon butter

2–3 tablespoons blanched almonds, halved

1–2 teaspoons ground cinnamon

SERVES 4

Preheat the oven to 180°C (350°F) Gas 4.

Put the couscous in an ovenproof dish. Stir the salt into the warm water and pour it over the couscous. Stir once to make sure all the grains are submerged in the water, cover the dish with a clean tea/dish towel and leave the couscous to absorb the water for 10 minutes.

Rake a fork through the couscous to loosen the grains then, using your fingers, rub the oil into them, lifting the grains up into the air and letting them fall back into the dish to aerate them. Dot the top of the couscous with the butter, cover the dish with a piece of dampened baking paper and pop it into the preheated oven for 15 minutes to heat through.

Meanwhile, prepare the almonds for the top, if using. Melt the butter in a heavy-based pan, stir in the almonds and sauté over a medium heat until they begin to turn golden. Drain on paper towels.

Take the couscous out of the oven and fluff up the grains with a fork, then tip it onto a serving dish, piling it into a pyramid. If using, scatter the almonds over and around the couscous pyramid. Rubbing the cinnamon between your fingers, dust it over the top, or in lines down the sides of the pyramid. Serve immediately.

Couscous with turmeric and ginger

You can make this couscous as spicy as you like by adding more chilli/chile or ginger. It goes well with both the sweet and the spicy tagines and it is delicious served on its own with a dollop of thick creamy yogurt and a Moroccan chutney or pickle.

500 g/2¾ cups couscous

1 teaspoon sea salt

600 ml/2½ cups warm water

2 tablespoons ghee or argan oil, or 1 tablespoon olive oil plus 1 tablespoon butter

a large thumb-sized piece of fresh ginger, peeled and very finely chopped

1 red chilli/chile, deseeded and finely chopped

2 teaspoons ground turmeric

a small bunch of fresh coriander/cilantro, finely chopped

sea salt and freshly ground black pepper

SERVES 4–6

Tip the couscous into a large bowl. Stir the salt into the warm water and pour it over the couscous. Stir once to make sure all the grains are submerged in the water, cover the bowl with a clean tea/dish towel and leave the couscous to absorb the water for 10 minutes. Rake the couscous with a fork to break up the grains.

Heat the ghee in a heavy-based saucepan, stir in the ginger and chilli/chile and sauté for 2–3 minutes, until they begin to colour. Add the turmeric and couscous and toss everything together, making sure it is thoroughly mixed. Toss in most of the coriander/cilantro and season with salt and pepper.

Tip the couscous into a serving dish, garnish with the rest of the coriander/cilantro and serve.

Couscous with braised fennel, courgette and orange

Couscous with cooked vegetables can be served as a side dish or on its own. With bursts of citrusy flavour, this couscous dish is a colourful and refreshing accompaniment to tagines and grills.

500 g/2¾ cups couscous

½ teaspoon sea salt

600 ml/2½ cups warm water

4 tablespoons olive oil

50 g/3½ tablespoons butter, cut into little pieces

2 fennel bulbs

1 courgette/zucchini

1–2 teaspoons aniseed seeds

grated zest of 1 orange and freshly squeezed juice of 2 oranges

1 tablespoon honey

1 tablespoon orange blossom water

sea salt and freshly ground black pepper

SERVES 4

Preheat the oven to 180°C (350°F) Gas 4.

Put the couscous in an ovenproof dish. Stir the salt into the warm water and pour it over the couscous. Stir once to make sure all the grains are submerged in the water, cover the dish with a clean tea/dish towel and leave the couscous to absorb the water for 10 minutes.

Rake a fork through the couscous to loosen the grains then, using your fingers, rub 2 tablespoons of the oil into them, lifting the grains up into the air and letting them fall back into the dish to aerate them. Dot the top of the couscous with half of the butter, cover the dish with a piece of dampened baking paper and pop it into the preheated oven for 10–15 minutes to heat through.

Trim the fennel bulbs, remove the outer leaves and quarter them. Trim off the courgette/zucchini ends, cut it in half, then slice it lengthways.

Heat the remaining oil in the base of a tagine or in a heavy-based saucepan, stir in the aniseed and grated orange zest and sauté for 1–2 minutes, until fragrant. Toss in the quartered fennel bulbs, then pour in the orange juice. Put the lid on the tagine and cook gently for 3–4 minutes.

Add the courgette/zucchini to the tagine, along with the remaining butter and toss through. Season with salt and pepper and drizzle the honey over the top. Cover and cook for another 3–4 minutes, until the fennel and courgette/zucchini are tender. Remove the lid and boil any remaining liquid for 3–4 minutes, until it caramelizes a little, then splash the orange blossom water over the vegetables.

Pile the couscous into a mound on a shallow serving dish and spoon the fennel and courgette/zucchini over and around it. Drizzle the caramelized juice over the top and serve.

Couscous tfaia

A traditional 'tfaia' embodies several features – onions, saffron and sultanas or raisins. Other ingredients can be added but this is tfaia at its simplest. It livens up a simple dish of couscous and can be served with most tagines.

350 g/2 cups couscous

1 teaspoon sea salt

400 ml/1⅔ cups warm water

25 g/2 tablespoons butter, cut into little pieces

For the tfaia

2–3 tablespoons ghee or smen (see page 12), or 1 tablespoon olive oil plus 1 tablespoon butter

4 onions, finely sliced

a large thumb-sized piece of fresh ginger, peeled and chopped

4 cinnamon sticks

2 tablespoons sultanas/ golden raisins

1 teaspoon saffron threads, soaked in 4 tablespoons water

2 tablespoons honey

sea salt and freshly ground black pepper

a bunch of fresh coriander/ cilantro, finely chopped, to garnish

SERVES 4

Preheat the oven to 180°C (350°F) Gas 4.

Put the couscous in an ovenproof dish. Stir the salt into the warm water and pour it over the couscous. Stir once to make sure all the grains are submerged in the water, cover the dish with a clean tea/dish towel and leave the couscous to absorb the water for 10 minutes.

Rake a fork through the couscous to loosen the grains then, using your fingers, rub the oil into them, lifting the grains up into the air and letting them fall back into the dish to aerate them. Dot the top of the couscous with the butter, cover the dish with a piece of dampened baking paper and pop it into the preheated oven for 15 minutes to heat through.

Meanwhile, heat the ghee in the base of a tagine or in a heavy-based saucepan, stir in the onions, ginger and cinnamon sticks and sauté for 2–3 minutes. Add the sultanas/ golden raisins and saffron, with its soaking water, cover the pan and cook gently for 8–10 minutes. Season with salt and pepper, stir in the honey and cook the tfaia gently for about 5 minutes.

Pile the couscous into a mound on a shallow serving dish, hollow out the top and spoon the tfaia into it. Garnish with the coriander/cilantro and serve.

Lemon couscous with roasted vegetables and lime

500 g/2¾ cups couscous

½ teaspoon sea salt

600 ml/2½ cups warm water

1–2 tablespoons olive oil

1 preserved lemon (see page 13), finely chopped

1 tablespoon butter, cut into little pieces

2 limes, cut into quarters

For the roasted vegetables

8 baby aubergines/eggplants, cut in half lengthways, keeping the stalk intact

2 courgettes/zucchini, halved and cut into quarters lengthways

2 (bell) peppers, deseeded and cut into quarters lengthways

4 garlic cloves, cut into 4 lengthways

a large thumb-sized piece of fresh ginger, peeled and cut into thin sticks

1–2 teaspoons sugar or honey

1–2 teaspoons finely chopped dried chilli/chile

100 ml/6 tablespoons olive oil

sea salt

SERVES 4–6

For this recipe, you can roast the vegetables in the oven or cut them into bite-sized chunks, thread them onto skewers, and grill them over a barbecue. Generally, peppers, aubergines/eggplants, courgettes/ zucchini, shallots and cherry tomatoes are used for roasting and grilling, but you can vary the mix with other seasonal vegetables. Serve with a dollop of yogurt or a drizzle of buttermilk, and a chutney, relish, or a crunchy salad.

Preheat the oven to 200°C (400°F) Gas 6.

Put all the vegetables in an ovenproof dish with the garlic and ginger. Add the sugar and chilli and toss everything together well. Pour over the oil, sprinkle with salt and put the vegetables in the preheated oven for about 50 minutes, turning them from time to time, until they are tender and nicely browned.

Meanwhile, put the couscous in an ovenproof dish. Stir the salt into the warm water and pour it over the couscous. Stir once to make sure all the grains are submerged in the water, cover the dish with a clean tea/dish towel and leave the couscous to absorb the water for 10 minutes.

Rake a fork through the couscous to loosen the grains then, using your fingers, rub the oil into them, lifting the grains up into the air and letting them fall back into the dish to aerate them. Toss in the Preserved Lemon and dot the top of the couscous with the butter, cover the dish with a piece of dampened baking paper and pop it into the preheated oven for 15 minutes to heat through.

To serve, tip the couscous onto a plate in a mound. Make a dip in the top and arrange the vegetables over and around the couscous. Spoon some of the roasting oil over the top of the mound and arrange the lime wedges around the edge to squeeze over the vegetables.

Saffron couscous with roasted coconut and pistachios

This simple couscous dish is light and fragrant and often served on its own between courses to stabilize the palate after spicy dishes. It can also be served alongside salads and dips as a starter, or as an accompaniment to grilled and roasted vegetable dishes.

350 g/2 cups couscous

1/2 teaspoon sea salt

a pinch of saffron threads

400 ml/1 2/3 cups warm water

3 tablespoons desiccated/dried shredded coconut

2 tablespoons olive oil

25 g/2 tablespoons butter, cut into little pieces

1–2 tablespoons finely ground pistachio nuts

freshly ground black pepper

SERVES 4

Preheat the oven to 180°C (350°F) Gas 4.

Put the couscous into an ovenproof dish.

Stir the salt and saffron into the warm water and leave to stand for 5 minutes so that the threads impart their yellow dye. Pour the saffron water over the couscous. Stir once to make sure all the grains are submerged in the water and the saffron threads are dispersed. Cover the dish with a clean tea/dish towel and leave the couscous to absorb the water for 10 minutes.

Meanwhile, roast the coconut in a small heavy-based frying pan/skillet until it begins to turn golden and emits a nutty aroma.

Rake a fork through the couscous to loosen the grains then, using your fingers, rub the oil into them, lifting the grains up into the air and letting them fall back into the dish to aerate them. Toss in the roasted coconut and season with pepper. Dot the top of the couscous with the butter, cover the dish with a piece of dampened baking paper and pop it into the preheated oven for 15 minutes to heat through.

Pile the couscous into a mound on a shallow serving dish and scatter the ground pistachio nuts over it, or in lines up and down the mound, and serve.

Lemon and orange couscous with walnuts and pomegranate seeds

Light with a citrus burst, this is a delightful couscous dish to serve with the sweet, honey-based tagines. You can also serve it cold by transforming it into a salad with the addition of finely chopped herbs and a light ginger dressing.

500 g/2¾ cups couscous

½ teaspoon sea salt

600 ml/2½ cups warm water

2 oranges

grated zest and freshly squeezed juice of 1 lemon

1–2 tablespoons olive oil

120 g/4 oz. toasted walnuts, roughly chopped

seeds of 1 pomegranate

sea salt and freshly ground black pepper

a small bunch of fresh flat-leaf parsley, roughly chopped, to garnish

SERVES 4–6

Preheat the oven to 180°C (350°F) Gas 4.

Put the couscous in an ovenproof dish. Stir the salt into the warm water and pour it over the couscous. Stir once to make sure all the grains are submerged in the water, cover the dish with a clean tea/dish towel and leave the couscous to absorb the water for 10 minutes.

Meanwhile, use a sharp knife to remove the peel and pith of 1 orange. Cut between the membranes to release the segments, then cut each segment in half and put them aside. Grate the zest of the other orange, then squeeze it to extract the juice. Combine the lemon and orange zest in a bowl and combine the lemon and orange juice in a separate bowl.

Rake a fork through the couscous to loosen the grains then, using your fingers, rub the oil into them, lifting the grains up into the air and letting them fall back into the dish to aerate them. Rub the orange and lemon zest into the grains, cover the couscous dish with a piece of dampened baking paper and pop it into the preheated oven for 10 minutes to heat through.

Remove the dish from the oven and toss in the orange and lemon juice, orange segments (reserve a few for garnishing), walnuts and half the pomegranate seeds. Season the couscous with salt and pepper, cover with the baking paper and return the dish to the oven for another 10 minutes.

Pile the couscous into a mound on a shallow serving dish. Scatter the parsley over the top and garnish with the reserved orange segments and pomegranate seeds. Serve immediately.

Couscous with dried fruit and nuts

This impressive-looking couscous dish is delicious served as a course on its own with yogurt or as an accompaniment to grills and roasts. You can vary the dried ingredients, but make sure the couscous grains are packed with lots of nutty and fruity goodness.

500 g/2¾ cups couscous

1 teaspoon sea salt

a pinch of saffron threads

600 ml/2½ cups warm water

3 tablespoons sunflower oil

2 tablespoons ghee or smen (see page 12), or 1 tablespoon olive oil plus 1 tablespoon butter

2 tablespoons blanched almonds, cut into slivers

1 tablespoon shelled pistachio nuts

1 tablespoon pine nuts

120 g/scant 1 cup ready-to-eat dried apricots, cut into slivers

120 g/scant 1 cup dried dates, chopped

2 tablespoons (zante) currants or raisins

2 teaspoons ground cinnamon

3 tablespoons icing/confectioners' sugar

SERVES 4–6

Preheat the oven to 180°C (350°F) Gas 4.

Put the couscous in an ovenproof dish. Stir the salt and saffron into the warm water and pour it over the couscous. Stir once to make sure all the grains are submerged in the water, cover the dish with a clean tea/dish towel and leave the couscous to absorb the water for 10 minutes.

Rake a fork through the couscous to loosen the grains then, using your fingers, rub the oil into them, lifting the grains up into the air and letting them fall back into the dish to aerate them.

Heat the ghee in a heavy-based saucepan, stir in most of the almond slivers and sauté for 1–2 minutes. Toss in the pistachios, pine nuts and dried fruit and cook for a further 1–2 minutes, then pour the mixture into the dish with the couscous and toss through. Cover the dish with a piece of dampened baking paper and pop it into the preheated oven for 15 minutes to heat through.

Pile the couscous into a mound on a large, shallow serving dish and sprinkle with the cinnamon and sugar – this is usually done in alternate stripes up and down the mound. Toast the reserved almond slivers and scatter them over the top, to serve.

Parsley, walnut and tomato salad with pomegranate syrup

Parsley, or mixed herb, salads are quite common accompaniments to tagines as they cut the spice and refresh the palate. The only dressing employed in this salad is the thick, treacle-coloured pomegranate syrup made from sour pomegranates and available in Asian and North African stores. As a substitute, you could use the juice of half a lemon combined with one tablespoon of fortified balsamic vinegar. Serve with toasted flatbreads or to accompany a dip.

a large bunch of fresh flat-leaf parsley

2–3 tablespoons shelled walnuts

2–3 tomatoes

1–2 green chillies/chiles, deseeded and finely chopped

1 red onion, finely chopped

2 tablespoons pomegranate syrup

sea salt

SERVES 4

Chop the parsley leaves and stalks – not too fine, not too coarse – and tip them into a shallow serving bowl. Chop the walnuts – again not too fine, so that they have a bite to them – and add them to the serving bowl.

Scald the tomatoes in a pan of boiling water for 2–3 seconds, drain and refresh under running cold water to loosen the skins. Peel and quarter the tomatoes, scoop out and discard the seeds and chop them coarsely. Add the tomatoes to the bowl along with the chillies/chiles and scatter the onion over the top.

Drizzle the pomegranate syrup over the salad and season well with salt. Leave the salad to sit for 15–20 minutes to allow the onion juice to weep into the salad. Gently toss the salad and serve.

Orange and date salad with chillies and preserved lemon

A delight to the eyes and the palate, this is a delicious salad to serve with any type of dish, particularly other spicy dishes. The four ingredients encompass the four pillars of Moroccan culinary tradition – sweet, salty, hot and fruity.

3–4 ripe, sweet oranges

150 g/1 cup moist, dried dates

2–3 tablespoons orange blossom water

½ preserved lemon (see page 13)

1 red chilli/chile, deseeded and finely chopped

SERVES 4

Peel the oranges, removing as much of the pith as possible. Place the oranges on a plate to catch the juice and finely slice them into circles or half moons. Remove and discard the seeds, then put the orange slices in a shallow bowl.

Slice the dates finely lengthways and scatter them over the oranges. Pour the orange blossom water over the oranges and dates, cover the bowl and leave for 15 minutes so that the flavours mingle and the dates soften.

Cut the preserved lemon in half, remove all the flesh, seeds and pith and finely slice or chop the peel. Scatter the preserved lemon and chilli/chile over the oranges and dates and gently toss to mix up the flavours a little before serving.

Grapefruit and pomegranate salad with rosewater

Deliciously refreshing on a hot day and a tremendous palate soother after a hot and spicy tagine or couscous dish, this salad is full of texture – juicy and crunchy – and pretty to look at, too.

2 pink or ruby grapefruit

1 white grapefruit

2 ripe pomegranates

2 tablespoons rosewater

sea salt

1 tablespoon finely shredded
   fresh mint leaves, to garnish

SERVES 4

Using a small sharp knife, remove the skins and pith from the grapefruit, then carefully cut down in between the membranes to release the fruit segments – catch the juice in a bowl below to add to the salad. Arrange the grapefruit segments in a shallow serving bowl and splash the juice over them.

Cut the pomegranates into quarters, bend each one backwards and scoop out the seeds, removing the pith – again, do this over a bowl to catch the juice. Scatter the seeds and juice over the grapefruit in the serving bowl.

Splash the rosewater over the salad, sprinkle with a little salt and garnish with the mint leaves. Serve chilled, or at room temperature.

Index

Picture credits

All photography © Ryland Peters & Small unless otherwise indicated:

Martin Brigdale
Pages 18–21, 25, 29–38, 44, 48–55

Peter Cassidy
Pages 2, 14, 17, 22, 26, 43, 47, 57, 118

Steve Painter
Pages 8–10, 12, 13, 15, 41, 59, 60–72, 75–101, 105–117, 119–141

© Steve Painter: Pages 1, 3–6, 11, 40, 56, 74, 102–103